THE RECYCLED TEEN

THE RECYCLED TEEN

A recycled teenager finds his way
onto a ship to serve God

JIM DEAN

The Recycled Teen
Published by Jim Dean
with Castle Publishing Ltd
New Zealand

© 2025 Jim Dean

ISBN 978-0-473-74600-1 (Softcover)
ISBN 978-0-473-74601-8 (ePUB)
ISBN 978-0-473-74602-5 (Kindle)

Production & Typesetting:
Andrew Killick
Castle Publishing Services
www.castlepublishing.co.nz

Cover Design:
Dreamcraft Experience
hello@dreamcraftexperience.com.au

Unless otherwise indicated, all Scripture taken from
the New King James Version®.
Copyright © 1982 by Thomas Nelson, Inc.
Used by permission. All rights reserved.

For other versions used,
see the Notes section at the end of this book.

ALL RIGHTS RESERVED

No part of this publication may be reproduced,
stored in a retrieval system, or transmitted
in any form or by any means, electronic, mechanical,
photocopying, recording or otherwise,
without prior written permission from the author.

FOREWORD

Behind any team ventures, missions, church life or events etc – there are always the people you may not see, the unsung heroes of the faith! They are rarely upfront or visible but are reliably serving behind the scenes helping to make things happen. Jim Dean is certainly one of those people. Reading through this book was a bit of a walk down memory lane for me as a lot of the ventures Jim served in I either was involved with personally or knew those who were.

Jim's a faithful man of God with servant hands and a big heart – he has an affectionate laugh and a great "can-do" attitude.

Enjoy the read and be inspired by Jim's life-story.

Bruce Benge

CONTENTS

Introduction	9
1. Early Life	11
2. New Farm, Marriage and Family	19
3. Hūnua and Life Changes	27
4. Mercy Missions	41
5. Hong Kong	57
6. New Zealand Furlough	87
7. England	93
8. Africa Mercy	107
9. Full Circle Returning Home	149
10. Final Thoughts	155
Acknowledgements	159
Notes	161

INTRODUCTION

When I turned 50 in 1988, my eldest daughter, Cherry, gave me a T-shirt with "Recycled Teen" emblazoned across the front. It was quite fun to wear it down the main street and watch the grins spread on people's faces as they read it. The memory has lasted long after the shirt has worn out.

At nearly sixty, I started writing this story and although I am now in my eighties, I still do not feel old – well, maybe a little. A teenager – starting out life with many adventures ahead, maybe a gap year, maybe an overseas adventure and certainly a few trials ahead. I think the appeal of the shirt was that, in my fifties, I became a teenager of sorts in my journey with God. Starting with trials and sadness, to becoming keen and enthusiastic, knowing everything and nothing – so much to learn and experience in my journey ahead.

This book has been in progress for over twenty years. As an avid reader myself, I have been inspired by so many Christians – both in person and in stories I have read. I am often asked about my time as a Missionary serving God.

As a Christian, I used to wonder how the Israelites managed to turn away from God during the forty years that they spent in the Wilderness, after God had done so many miracles for them, during their escape from the Egyptians. One day it came to me that I was no better, and that I tended to forget all the wonderful things that He had done for me, so I felt it was necessary for me to write down as many as I could remember. I used my time after returning from Hong Kong to document as many moments as possible, which is where this book began its life.

As I started writing, many more memories kept coming back to me as I tried to be obedient to Him.

I will remember the works of the Lord;
Surely I will remember Your wonders of old.
I will also meditate on all Your work,
And talk of Your deeds.
(Psalm 77:11-12)

I would like to encourage you, and say that anyone is able to do any of the things shared in this book, and even more. To overcome your fears and doubts, simply invite Jesus Christ into your heart and be obedient to Him. While it may take time, if you set aside your concerns, excuses, and pride, you will be able to achieve these things.

As for me, I am still a work in progress.

ONE

EARLY LIFE

I was born on February 5th, 1938, at Te Awamutu in the North Island of New Zealand, and our family lived on Waikeria Road with the farm backing onto a prison property. I had the usual childhood, in some ways quite spoilt. I started school when I was five, travelling in a bus seven miles to primary and intermediate schools. Mum used to insist that I wore shoes to school, but as most of the other boys did not, I used to hide my shoes at the gate and collect them on the way home.

As I grew up during World War II, there were many shortages. For example, we made our own butter using a churn. I can remember turning and turning that churn. I learned to shoot with a .22 rifle and used to hunt rabbits. I would usually shoot about eight rabbits, which was as many as I could carry home. They were a valuable source of meat, as meat was rationed during the war and afterwards. I must say that I never enjoyed eating rabbit. We also had lots of bantam hens for eggs and sometimes we used the poor roosters for meat as well.

My father was a Fat Stock Buyer, buying animals for meat. He was supplied with a company car for the job. He owned a dairy farm and used to employ people to milk the cows. Later he had share milkers, who owned the cows but leased the farm from him.

Dad loved "breaking-in" horses and we always had several. Mind you, the words "breaking-in" were not how he usually did it. He used to make friends with them until they allowed him to ride them or use them for farm work, as in the early days we did not have tractors.

Around 1948 there was a Polio epidemic. We were not allowed to go to school for about three months, and my younger brother Ron missed a whole year of school. Incidentally, my mother had contracted Polio as a little girl and had one leg shorter than the other, and many health issues because of it.

In 1949 Dad went to the north coast of Gisborne, on New Zealand's North Island, in a new Ford car to buy hundreds of cattle. There had been a major tidal wave (tsunami) and most of the bridges had been washed out and we had to ford many of the rivers. Dad bought cattle all the way up the coast and then sent several drovers to gather them up to drive them on foot all the way to Horotiu near Hamilton. The mobs travelled about four miles a day and grazed the grass along the sides of the road, and consequently put on a lot of weight during the trip to the freezing meat works. Dad used to visit the drovers about once a week to deliver provisions to them, and to check on the cattle. The total distance the cows travelled was approximately 350 miles (nearly 600 kilometres).

In 1952 I was sent to Kings College, a church boarding school in Ōtāhuhu (Auckland). Just after I started there I got sick and ended up in the school hospital for two weeks, missing out on learning all the school rules that the rest of the students were taught. As a result, I was frequently in trouble, and got the nickname of "Cast Iron Bum," due to the many canings I received. I was an average student, and did not pass my School Certificate.

Early Life

I did the Anglican confirmation classes, but ultimately I decided not to be Confirmed while at school. I made some very good friends while I was there, some of whom have stayed in contact to this day.

I was a bit frustrated at school as I loved wide open spaces. When the school terms ended, I couldn't get back to the farm quickly enough where I particularly enjoyed horse riding in its various forms. My next love was machinery, how it all worked, maintenance and operation.

In my last year at Kings College, I went to hear an evangelist called Billy Graham and as I sat in the Auckland Town Hall listening to him, something strange happened to me. When he called for people to go forward to accept Jesus into their lives, I felt compelled to but tried to ignore the feeling. I had to hold onto my chair to stop myself from going forward. I was quite frightened that God would take me up chair and all. But as I sat there, I silently prayed to accept Jesus into my heart – "in my closet" (my chair).

After I left school, I forgot about what I had done. But although I didn't realise it then, it was to have a major effect on my life much later. At that time I got the gift of tongues, although I did not know what it was. I used to go around the farm singing in a language that I did not understand. I remember that it made me feel peaceful.

I was very fortunate to have a loving father, who took me with him whenever he was able. He spent a lot of time teaching me as much as I would absorb. In fact, he tried to pass on to me all that he knew. He also used to encourage me to participate in any outside training sessions. His manner of teaching was that he would show me how to do it, and then he would encourage me to try and do it. It didn't seem to matter to him if I made a mistake while I was learning, but if I was certain I could do it, and didn't ask for help, I was in trouble if I made a mistake then.

In 1952 Dad allowed me to buy an old crawler tractor, it was an International T20. Dad got a blade built for it by Wally Bedford in Kihikihi. We used it for digging out stumps on our Pirongia farm, also for making tracks for access, or clearing fire breaks and fence lines.

In 1954 I left school and started to work on the family farm at Pirongia, mostly doing development work, stumping, fencing, clearing gorse, creating tracks and metalling them. I also used to do a bit of contract work for other people.

The Pirongia farm was 18 miles from our home farm and we used to drive back and forth each day. We often used to leave home at 4 am and on the way there we would call into a bakery to buy our lunch. The smell of hot bread was absolute torture, and it was very hard to resist eating it before lunch time. Dad and I worked together and we enjoyed each other's company.

I started driving trucks on the road as soon as I turned 18, and have continued to drive them on and off to the present day. I helped Dad with his stock buying business where he taught me to buy cattle from the sale yards. After a time I became quite proficient at estimating the weights of the cattle. We finally gave up the business after the United States rejected a New Zealand shipment of cattle for being contaminated with DDT (an agricultural pesticide now considered to be carcinogenic). It was a very worrying time for us, as we had many thousands of pounds worth of cattle in transit at the time. Fortunately, none of the rejected shipments were ours.

Often we had a need to take a wild, but promising, horse, training it to become tame and able to be ridden. I was working

Early Life

with a five-year-old stallion that had been incorrectly "broken-in," so I used to ride him, hanging on tight on with my knees. One time, he reared backwards – the opposite to what he normally did, I fell off and he rolled down over me, and I injured my ankle quite badly. Incidentally, this ankle has given me grief all of my life!

To keep myself out of trouble I took myself off to a trip to the South Island in my dad's car, a Morris Minor. I made it as far south as Dunedin. After a few days, I decided to catch the inter-island ferry from Lyttelton in the South Island, to Wellington on the North Island. This was an overnight sail on the ferry *Maori* and I thoroughly enjoyed it. An interesting point to note about this ship was that she was built in Newcastle upon Tyne (UK) where I later ended up. At the time I travelled, the *Maori* was on its second-to-last ferry crossing, and then was purchased by YWAM (Youth With A Mission) with the intent for it to be converted into a hospital ship. I was interested in the concept at the time but did not know much more.

In July 1956 I started 50/50 share-milking on Dad's farm south of Te Awamutu, which I continued for the next five years, going from a 74 cow herd to 100 cows plus replacements, on 96 acres. This was the first time that I had so much work I needed to employ extra labour. One of the first people that I employed was unsuitable, and because he was much older, he tried to take advantage of my youth. After much discussion with Dad, I was told to sack him. Dad offered me advice, but he was adamant that it was my responsibility. So I learnt a very valuable, but uncomfortable lesson, which has stood me in good stead ever after. I have never found it easy to lay someone off.

Towards the end of this period my younger brother, Ron, came to work with me. As he became more involved with the farm, I started to do outside contracting, mostly spraying, loading and cultivation. I was also involved in part-time truck driving for the local carriers.

In my first year on the farm, I joined the local Young Farmers Club (YFC) and was later elected to be Club Reporter, Vice Chairman, and finally, Chairman. As Chairman of the club, I was automatically made a representative of the Waipā District Committee, which was comprised of ten clubs. I was elected Vice Chairman, and the following year, District Chairman. As a club reporter, one of my duties was to help the local printer prepare a monthly newsletter where I learned about typesetting.

My first official function as District Chairman, at 18 years of age, was to chair a meeting of 400 people, including many dignitaries, at a formal dinner in the Te Awamutu town hall. I was so nervous that I stuttered and stammered my speech of welcome. I unintentionally made everyone laugh, but I felt they were laughing with me, and after that I was alright!

It was through the YFC that I became involved in small bore rifle shooting. I was asked to shoot in an inter-club competition, and was most disgusted when my score was only 78% and the rifle club members were making nearly 100%. I became very determined to do at least as well as them. It took me several months to shoot my first 100% score, and by that time I had joined the rifle club.

I went on to hold several executive positions over the years on the rifle club committee, among them becoming Captain for the Waikato team. Eventually I managed to win quite a number of competitions. When we moved to Ōtorohanga, we started a small-bore rifle club there on the farm.

It was about that time that I tried out for the North Island Small Bore Rifle team. On my way to the competition, I came across an accident on the road, and it was my friend's father. He was injured and carted off to hospital in an ambulance. It upset me badly and I could not shoot as well as I normally did. I missed out on representing the North Island by one place.

As our farm on Waikeria Road was reaching its full potential, Dad decided we needed a bigger farm, and after a lot of searching we found one in Ōtorohanga. Dad then sold the Waikeria Road farm in 1960, and the family moved to a 191-acre dairy farm at Ōtewā. To ease family pressures, my brother Ron and I, and whoever was working for us, lived in the second house on the property. It was built of corrugated iron, with an outdoor toilet and was very basic.

This new dairy farm at Ōtewā needed a lot of development work. Ron, myself and the other lads did a lot of stumping, fencing, roading, draining, re-grassing, extending the cowshed, and we built a large shed. After we had been there for a year, I sold my herd of cows to Ron and put more emphasis on my contracting work.

We felled a lot of trees on the farm for posts and carted them to Hamilton to be treated, and then carted them back again. One day I was carting a load of 220 dry posts to Hamilton on a three-ton truck. A traffic police officer pulled me up and asked how much weight I thought I had. I replied, "About one and a half tons," and he laughed at me sarcastically, then put the truck over the scales. It was slightly less than I had estimated, and he was not very pleased, so he inspected everything that he could, and couldn't find anything wrong. On the way back on the same day, I had a load of 80 posts straight out of the treatment kiln and they would have weighed well over three tons and would probably have been well overweight. I passed the same policeman, and this time he just glared at me but did not stop me for inspection. Phew!

The Recycled Teen

At this time I continued with my contracting and other casual work when I wasn't needed on the farm. I did quite a lot of truck driving for a local carrier as well a little bit of sheep shearing on contract.

We were fortunate to have a new neighbour, John Garret, move in, who was very skilled in engineering and radio repairs. He was generous with his time and taught us all a lot. During the Second World War he had been a Desert Rat and had been stationed on the Island of Leros in the Mediterranean. He encouraged us to build or modify a lot of our own machinery. When we asked him how we could repay him, he said that he wanted and needed nothing, and suggested that we pass on our knowledge to others. Later I was to discover that this is a very important Christian principle that I have continued practising throughout my life.

One of the projects that stands out was that we bought an old generator and John helped us to convert it into a welder, driven by a Forson Major engine. This welder was not very successful so we ended up buying a Lincoln Welder, and again with John's help and some kiwi ingenuity, we managed to drive it with a Wisconsin engine to improve its capabilities.

I developed new friendships in the district and through one of them, eventually met my wife. Two friends and I used to drive to Hamilton on Saturday nights to go to dances and meet the girls.

TWO
NEW FARM, MARRIAGE AND FAMILY

In 1964 I met a young lady named Carol Smith, who was nursing at Cassel Private Hospital in Hamilton. A mutual friend set us up on a blind date. As I was waiting to meet her, a young woman walked into the room before me, and then a voice behind me said, "There is the girl that you are going to marry." I quickly looked around, but there was no one behind me, and as I looked back the voice repeated it. I am absolutely convinced it was God speaking to me. Though Carol was unofficially engaged to someone else and uninterested in going out with me, I persisted when I would normally have walked away. And after several refusals, we started going out together and we were married on May 15, 1965.

I worked for five months on a 550-acre sheep and cattle (beef) farm in Kopaki, Northern King Country. Two weeks before I married, I purchased this farm from an Indian family who had been very helpful and provided room and board while I refurbished some of the fences. During my stay with them I learned to enjoy a good curry. When it came to the purchase, they would not allow me to put an option on the farm. They insisted on a cash settlement the day I took over the property. They wanted full payment in cash, but I only had a bank draft which they initially refused to accept. Fortunately their accountant advised them a bank draft was acceptable. Once the sale was completed, the family then wanted the bank to give them cash and they became upset when the bank did not have the full amount of cash on hand.

The Kopaki farm was rolling hill country – some very steep – three miles long with plenty of natural water, including a nice stream flowing through it. While it required substantial development work, this challenge appealed to me. Much of the work could be done by stock management, and cropping. A great deal of fencing needed to be done and we erected about 12-15 miles of fencing over the time that we owned it. We had felled approximately 50 acres of very tall Tea Tree using a crew of Fijian-Indian workers. We then burned and grass-seeded that cleared paddock. The seeding was done with an aeroplane, flying low at 90 miles per hour. The pilot's skill was such that the seed was never more than a metre and a half from where it was supposed to land.

After the grass had come up, the paddock suddenly grew a lot of field mushrooms, so many in fact, that I used to take my short wheel base Landrover and completely fill the back of it with them. I took them into the local hospital and gave them to the nurses who were raising money as part of a Queen's Carnival for the hospital. Sometimes I would get two loads per day, a huge amount of mushrooms!

This was a very special and happy time in my life, even though we were very cashflow poor. We went to Kopaki conservatively budgeting for five years of losses, but because of a drastic fall in wool prices five months later, we only made one very small profit in the first eight years. We were very fortunate though, for we were able to sell our first wool clip before the prices dropped.

This one sale made all the difference to our future. Some who had taken out mortgages on similar-sized farms had to walk off their farms at a later date due to debt. At one stage things were going so badly that I approached the Mortgagee (bank) and told him that I was unable to meet the principal repayments, but would be able to continue the interest payments. I was unsure how this would be received. Fortunately he was quite happy about it, as many farmers had been unable to pay anything.

We had very good neighbours in that area, and we all worked closely together. When we first moved in, several of the people turned up to welcome us, bringing cakes and other goodies. If one of us was sick, the rest of the neighbours would gather around to help out. We often worked together with our major jobs, such as hay making.

During this time we were blessed with three lovely daughters, Cherry, Sandra and Joanne. My mother was particularly delighted that we had produced three girls – as I learned much later, she had endured several miscarriages of female babies herself. We made many friends among the community, and attended the local church at Bennydale.

About the same time Carol and I became involved with the Social Welfare Department, and we worked as volunteer social workers. We were asked to supervise several young people who had been in trouble with the law. I also used to employ boys who had been in trouble with the law, on the farm. Most of them spent at least a year with us, and one stayed for as long as three years.

The Welfare Department also asked me to become a member of the local Children's Board. This involved a group of four of us dealing with children up to the age of 13, who had been in trouble with the police. We had very few powers of discipline, but it was a good way of dealing with the children as in most cases it kept them out of the Magistrate's Court. One of the advantages that we had over the Magistrate's Court was that we could compel the parents to attend if needed. This enabled us to deal with family situations that helped to stop the children re-offending.

Some of the cases were quite humorous, such as when a ten-year-old partially blocked a main highway with an old sofa because he was bored, on a straight stretch of road that had light traffic. When a driver in an expensive car had to get out to remove it, he yelled at the youngster frightening him. The boy then threw stones at the car breaking a light, so the police were called. It transpired that there was nothing for the youngster to do in this former milling village, so we found out that he liked working on mechanical things. In the same village there was an old man who used to repair small motors for his neighbours. So we arranged for the boy to work with him, and he gave no further trouble.

Another case was a family with thirteen children. The father had a good job, but half of his children had been involved in car theft, conversion, and joyriding. We discovered that this always happened in the evenings, so we asked the parents what they were doing at that time. They were going to the local pub at 6.00 pm, giving the children money to buy food from the local fish shop and leaving them in the car until 10.30 pm. Understandably, the bored kids got up to mischief. We suggested to the parents that they buy their beer and take it home to drink it where they could keep a closer eye on the kids. Thankfully, the rest of the family avoided further trouble during my time on the board.

Early on at Kopaki I built a workshop on the farm, and put

New Farm, Marriage and Family

a pit in it so that I could service vehicles and work underneath them. Eventually, I needed to do my own farmwork during the early morning and late afternoon hours, because I would be so busy repairing and servicing my neighbours' machinery. I never charged for this repairwork, except for the parts. In return, the neighbours would help me with my own farmwork. At times, I got jobs that I did not know how to do, so I used to go and sit on a stump and meditate, then I would figure out how to repair whatever was broken.

While mowing a paddock, my neighbour, David, struck a hidden stump at high speed, bending the sickle mower's framework and making it unusable. Sitting on the stump and contemplating this problem, we came up with a solution. We attached the mower to my shed and used the tractor in reverse to bend it slowly back. This solved the problem, as well as moving the shed foundation 18 inches!

Although I had some ideas about overseas travel when I first left school, I had lost all desire to do so, and was quite content to stay on the farm, except for some short holidays around New Zealand. When the three girls were quite small, Carol convinced me that we should go to Australia for a family holiday. Much to my surprise, I really enjoyed it. One of my favourite memories of the trip was seeing my three girls all lined up outside a Darrell Lea chocolate shop in Melbourne, with wide open mouths, huge grins and ginormous lollipops. After that trip we all caught the travel bug. We have had the good fortune to visit many other countries since then.

In the 1980s we had considered emigrating to Australia to buy a banana farm. I arranged a trip to look at some farms with my dad, this was to be his first flight on an aeroplane at 77 years old. Prior to this, the highest above the ground he had been was being bucked off a horse! It was while staying in motels during our travels, that one morning I discovered Dad on his knees praying. I asked him what was the matter and he told me that almost all his life he had done that. I felt so ashamed as I had not had that sort of dedication.

While Dad and I were away on that trip, Carol looked after the farm. It was very wet that winter, and Carol had slid off the steep tracks with the Land Rover and had been rescued by the neighbours. When I returned, I was quite ill for two weeks, so Carol had to continue managing the farm. I made a decision to sell the farm as I did not want to lose Carol in a farm accident. I made the decision to sell the farm in early 1980, and fortunately were allowed to rent the house back for as long as we needed it. Wisely, Carol suggested that we not move to Australia as both sets of our parents were elderly, and in not very good health. This proved to be very good advice.

While we looked for other suitable farms, I took a job driving logging trucks and transporters. It amazed me how long it took to become skilled in the work, especially as I had driven many different sorts of trucks and trailers over the years. I enjoyed the work as I did not have any business responsibilities to worry about.

While driving trucks, I had a challenging one-way road to navigate, so I would ask God to let me know when other vehicles were approaching. He would instruct me to pull off the road, and sure enough, a vehicle would come by just a few minutes later. The only time I encountered oncoming traffic was when I was transporting an oversized load with a police escort stopping traffic. Another driver had bypassed the road block and met me on a blind corner, leaving them with no choice but to veer into the ditch. The police later had a talk with that driver. Another route I took frequently wound through multiple farms, requiring me to open and close 13 gates each way. I became quite skilled at estimating my load length to minimise any extra steps.

We ended up looking at many different farms over a very large area. We had written down our requirements before we started, and after much searching, eventually found a suitable place at Hūnua, just 40 minutes from the International Airport and central Auckland. After searching through more than 100 other farms, we finally discovered the Hūnua farm in South Auckland.

THREE
HŪNUA AND LIFE CHANGES

And we know that all things work together for good to those who love God, to those who are the called according to His purpose. (Romans 8:28)

We moved to Hūnua in 1980, I thought, to semi-retire on a smaller farm of 167 acres. For a start, I quite enjoyed having a more relaxed life, but not for long. I started looking for jobs around the farm, and it wasn't long before I ran out of things to do.

One of the activities we had enjoyed as a family was being members in the local theatre groups both in Te Kūiti and then Hūnua. Carol was often involved with music, and even wrote an entire play, and my talents were used in stage managing and props.

Carol suggested that I try working in real estate. So without much hope I applied to work for a real estate agency, and found that I needed to pass some exams before I could begin. This was quite a hurdle for me as I had never done particularly well in exams, but I passed without any trouble. For the next three years I worked as a farm salesman with reasonable success. I continued to run the farm as well, with some casual help. It was a very hard time on my family, as I was at every one's beck and call and if it wasn't real estate, it was the farm. There were two reasons that caused me to leave the real estate industry, the first was that I was seldom free to spend time with my family. The second was that although I tried to do my job with total honesty, I found that I wasn't trusted, even by close personal friends, *just because I was working in real estate*! I decided to stop selling property for that reason.

While shearing sheep for a friend one day, he asked me to buy his wool. Selling the wool was difficult for him, as his business demanded all his time. Reluctantly, I agreed to purchase the wool. A friend who worked at a large New Zealand stock firm then arranged for me to receive training in wool classing. He also personally taught me a great deal about the trade. Looking back, I'm surprised I did so well, given my limited knowledge of wool at the time.

A few days later, another friend requested that I buy his wool as well. This marked the start of a business venture that occupied me for the next seven years. I most likely would have continued in the wool trade had God not intervened and asked me to give it up – which was a struggle for me at the time.

In March 1990 Carol left me. What started as a trial separation developed into a full breakup. I knew I had made a lot of mistakes, but it didn't help me with the devastation that I felt. At first, I just wanted to shut myself away and see no one, then some wonderful things happened, although I initially did not see it that way. A friend, Rick Van Miltenberg, heard what had happened and he came to see me even though I didn't want company. As I tried to shut the door in his face, I inadvertently jammed his toe in the door as I didn't want him to come in. Fortunately he persisted and patiently sat and listened to me pour out all my hurt, then he asked to pray with me. As he prayed about the situation, he prayed the scripture from John 14, verse 27:

Peace I leave with you, My peace I give to you; not as the world gives do I give to you. Let not your heart be troubled, neither let it be afraid. (John 14:27)

After the prayer, I had the most incredible peace that I had ever known. After Rick had left, I felt that I could re-read a letter that Carol had sent me, that I had been avoiding. Though I thought that I may have been unduly negative, re-reading the letter I immediately lost that wonderful peace. Rick rang a couple of days later to see how I was, and prayed that scripture again, of course with the same marvellous result. Rick remained in my life, and continued to lead me towards a relationship with Christ.

Then another friend turned up and offered to pray with me every Thursday morning at 6 am. I found out later that he hated getting up that early in the morning, but he persisted for some time. One morning he prayed that friends would gather around me for support. When I arrived home, I found a note on the door saying that a friend had stopped by to see me, and that he would call back later, which he did. So many people visited me or rang me that day, it was incredible and this continued for some time. I heard similar testimony from others on Radio Rhema, our Christian radio station. The friendship, testimonies, worship, and teaching I experienced during this time not only aided my healing, but also deepened my relationship with Christ.

God led me through the Ten Commandments, prompting me to write down all the wrongs I had committed and considered in my life. I was shocked by the length of the list. When I asked God what I should do with it, I felt he wanted me to give it to Carol. This made me very vulnerable, as I had withdrawn trust from her. But it was God's way of showing Carol that I still trusted her.

Next, God asked me to forgive the person Carol had gone with. My initial response was a firm "no," but he gently persisted until I asked "how?" I knew a direct "I forgive you" wouldn't be accepted, so God gave me the right words, time and place to do it. Surprisingly, it was I who felt released, not the other person.

While on my way to collect wool one day, I received calls from two friends urging me to worship the Lord. Although I was still hurting from the recent separation and didn't feel like worshipping, I tried singing old hymns like "Onward Christian Soldiers" and "Praise God From Whom All Blessings Flow." Running late, I set off and put on worship tapes for the 18-mile drive. As I listened, I found myself crying uncontrollably. Somehow, I arrived at my client's place on time, my shirt soaked from the tears.

To my surprise, I didn't recall passing through the nearby village. Nor could I explain how I made it there so quickly. The story took an unexpected turn when I learned my client had just lost her husband in a tragic boating accident where his body was never recovered. Suddenly, I realised there were people far worse off than I was, which helped me come to terms with my own separation.

Around this time our middle daughter, Sandy, was engaged to be married to Graham. I felt so upset at the breakup of our marriage that I felt I would be unable to go to the wedding. When I told Sandy, she said, "Don't worry Dad, I understand, but I think you should think about it as I may be the only one you get to walk down the aisle," and went off and prayed for me.

A few days before the wedding I decided that I might be able to go after all, so I let her know, but told her I wouldn't speak at the wedding. Two days beforehand, Sandy came to me and asked me to say something about how God was involved in their lives. I was not sure that I could do it, but promised to pray about it. In the early hours of the morning of the wedding morning, God started to give me the exact words to say. I sat up, turned on the light and wrote them down. When I delivered those words at the wedding, I noticed the Master of Ceremonies looked decidedly put out. It turned out that I had spoken the exact words that he planned to say – he had also been praying about what to say.

Graham and Sandy were nearing completion of their degrees at Waikato University in Hamilton. Graham was due to graduate at this time, and I had been invited to his capping ceremony. The graduation took place in the evening, and afterwards, we all went out to dinner to celebrate.

By the time I started the eighty-mile drive home, it was quite late and I was feeling very tired. I had not been sleeping well, and had been working a lot and driving in the few days prior. As I was driving home, I was so tired that I found myself struggling to stay awake at the wheel, but was determined to get home, thinking finally I might get a good night's sleep. After I arrived home and got to bed, God repeatedly woke me saying that He wanted me to take some action. Finally at 4 am I got out of bed, knelt down, and said, "Whatever You want me to do God, I will try and do it." Then I slept soundly until 7 am, the longest continuous sleep since Carol's departure.

The next day, Rick called to check on me. As usual he prayed for me over the phone. But he stopped mid-prayer, and asked me if I would like to attend a baptism service at First Church in

Papakura the following Sunday evening. I said yes, as I had heard positive things about the church. Rick explained a new baptism pool had just been installed in the church. He then asked me directly if I would be baptised. I replied I wasn't sure, but would pray about it. I had been baptised as a baby, and wasn't sure about being baptised a second time. I decided to ask God to give me a sign from the minister's sermon at my local church on Sunday morning, similar to Gideon (Judges 6:36-40).

The minister taking the service did not agree with being re-baptised, and he delivered a sermon on "Taking Risks in God and Steps in Faith." However, I felt certain that God wanted me to be re-baptised. After that service, a friend invited me back for a cup of tea. As soon as I arrived, she started to talk about the struggle that my friend Rick had as to whether he should be baptised again, as he too had been baptised as a baby. She did not know that I had been thinking about this, so I believe it was God confirming what I already felt. So that Sunday evening I was baptised, and afterwards I felt I was a completely different person.

Many years later, as I was reading about John the Baptist in my Bible, I felt assured I was on the right path, as I learned about the disciples baptising believers again for them to receive the Holy Spirit.

> *He asked them, "Did you receive the Holy Spirit when you believed [in Jesus as the Christ]?" And they said, "No, we have not even heard that there is a Holy Spirit." And he asked, "Into what then were you baptized?" They said, "Into John's baptism." Paul said, "John performed a baptism of repentance, continually telling the people to believe in Him who was coming after him, that is, [to confidently accept and joyfully*

believe] in Jesus [the Messiah and Savior]." After hearing this, they were baptized [again, this time] in the name of the Lord Jesus. (Acts 19:2-5 AMP)

One night, I had a vivid dream about being pulled over by a traffic police officer on a rainy night. In the dream, I was driving faster than I should have been, and the car behind me clearly noticed my speed. The policeman pulled me over and led me into a nearby tavern, instructing me to wait there while he rode off on a motorcycle. Unsure whether to stay or leave, I decided to wait. Eventually, the policeman returned and went into the tavern, emerging with a lady who approached me and said, "You have left your socks on the floor." To my surprise, there were my socks, and also a pair belonging to the policeman, whose feet were larger than mine. Feeling remorseful and missing my wife Carol, I lay down on a bench and began to sob. Unexpectedly, the policeman then lay down beside me and held me, comforting me. In that moment, I realised it was not a policeman, but rather Jesus, who was embracing and reassuring me.

This dream was so profound that it still affects me to this day. An interpretation of the dream is that the policeman represents a perception of religion – with conformity, commandments and rules to follow, but the change in the dream to him becoming Jesus shows the comfort, care and protection that I was now finding in Him. The detail about the socks was significant, as I used to frustrate Carol by carelessly leaving my socks wherever I removed them, despite never meaning to upset her.

From being a person who liked to plan my work up to two years in advance, God brought me to a place where I just had to get through just one hour at a time. Initially this was difficult, but I finally came to enjoy it. In fact, one of the most exciting prayers was to ask God what He and I were going to do for the day. While often I had my own idea, God frequently had other plans. It was exhilarating – a bit like riding a roller coaster!

One night, I felt that God was asking me to give up my wool-buying business, and the next day Carol visited me, so I told her about it. She reminded me of a wise piece of advice – not to make major decisions while feeling down. This resonated with me, even though I had been prepared to immediately give up the business.

Nearly six months later, after completing a New Christian class run by a church elder, I took the group out for a meal. During the meal, I shared with them about God's call for me to give up wool buying. The elder's wife then said, "If God is asking you to do something, for goodness sake do it." It wasn't until I had been obedient to Him that He allowed me join Mercy Missions.

I used to consider myself a self-made man, proud of the assets I had worked hard to build. But one day as I sat on the front steps feeling very sorry for myself, over the death of a pet guinea pig, I had a heartfelt realisation. My three daughters and their spouses had borrowed my van for the day. I felt God reminding me of a tragedy a week prior where six youths had been killed on the same road driving a similar van. In that moment, I recognised without God's grace, I could have lost everything – my house, my farm and even my family. I immediately repented and asked for His forgiveness. The loss of the guinea pig had opened my eyes to understanding true fear and dependence on God.

Another day I was looking out of my lounge window, watching some magpies feeding happily on the lawn, when along came two much smaller birds, who proceeded to feed on the lawn. This angered the magpies who tried to chase them away. The little birds soon came back, and the magpies continued to try to chase them away. Eventually the magpies just stood and glared, and the little birds continued to feed. I was compelled to ask God what He was trying to show me. His response was that when we become annoyed with our circumstances or the people around us, we often fail to see the provision and blessings He has in store.

A friend called to check on me one day. After being assured that I was alright, he enthusiastically told me about a football match that he had been to. A few days later he rang again and I shared some of the things that Jesus had been doing in my life. He commented that I was always talking about God, and he was not impressed. I reminded him of the lengthy football discussion, and explained to him that since I had developed a relationship with Christ, I couldn't help but talk about Jesus, as He was more exciting to me than football.

About this time, I went to hear Delores Winder – an American woman who had experienced a miraculous healing – speak at East Presbyterian Church in Papakura. I remember listening to her address and felt compelled to be "baptised in the Spirit," and learn to speak in tongues. After the service, we went into another room where people prayed for us to receive these spiritual gifts. While others in the group received them, I did not. Feeling upset, I went back into the church and sat in my chair wondering why. I was unsure whether to leave and go home, or stay.

Before I could leave, two ladies from my local Hūnua church came up to me and introduced me to Delores. She asked questions about my family and then began to pray for me. Although I cannot remember exactly what she prayed, I know she asked

God to bring His healing to me. At some stage I started to cry and I couldn't stop. This lasted for 24 hours, and was upsetting to my youngest daughter who was living at home at that time. Concerned, she considered ringing Carol, but through my tears I said I was okay. The tears brought about a cleansing by God, and afterwards I felt like a changed person. I note that there were, and still are, many areas of my life that need work. And at this point, I remained unable to speak in tongues.

While visiting a local garage to arrange some repair work for my truck the following day, I sensed that the proprietor was distressed. He shared with me that his daughter and her unborn baby had been hospitalised with a mysterious illness. I offered to go home and pray for her but lacked the confidence to pray with him in person. He was grateful I was willing to pray. As I drove home I prayed, but not very deeply. At 1 am, I felt a strong urge to pray earnestly for this woman I had never met.

During my prayers, I sensed God telling me to address the issues in my own life before trying to help others.

> *Thou hypocrite, first cast out the beam out of thine own eye; and then shalt thou see clearly to cast out the mote out of thy brother's eye.* (Matthew 7:5, KJV)

This led me to pray for healing of my own painful knee problems that had been making it difficult to get in and out of my truck. From that day on, my knee issues greatly improved.

The next day when I took my truck to the garage to be repaired, the proprietor told me that he had woken up at 1 am, and felt a significant weight had been lifted. Remarkably his daughter recovered and delivered a healthy baby. It was an amazing testament to God!

I had long prayed privately for the gift of tongues, even asking evangelists and others to pray that I would receive it. I had read in the Bible about God giving good gifts to those who asked for them, and even got to the stage of doubting God's word on the subject. One day while talking to Walter Scheer, a teacher at the discipleship training school I attended, I confessed I could not speak in tongues. Walter gathered up some students, and decided to pray for all of us. As he prayed for me, he asked God to release the gift that He had already given me. To my joy, I started to pray in tongues. Walter seemed puzzled and told me I had been able to do so "for a long, long time." I asked what he meant, and he just repeated "a long, long time." He told me not to worry about it, and that God would tell me in due course.

Years later, while having "quiet time" in my room at Hang Fook Camp in Hong Kong, I felt God ask if I wanted to know when I had received the gift of tongues. I immediately replied yes, and He revealed it was at the Billy Graham meeting in Auckland where I had accepted Jesus into my heart without going forward to the stage.

During this period I continued to manage the farm and the wool-buying business, while also assisting my cousin Bill with his company, Industrial Auctions – which I really enjoyed. Bill, a fellow Christian, provided wonderful support through my personal difficulties. We often began our work with prayer, asking God for guidance for the day.

The nature of our work often required travel to different cities for several weeks at a time. I usually stayed in motels near the site so that I was able to work longer hours. Because of Christ's impact on my life, I was eager to learn more about Him. So on Sundays, I would leave the motel and ask God to direct me to the right church. God proved faithful, and each service

I attended was just what I needed at that time. I visited many different denominations, but that did not matter to me, as they were all Christians.

One day Bill and I were working together setting up an auction, and we got very upset with each other. The details have faded from my memory, but I do recall it was so serious that I intended to finish this auction, and then resign. I stamped off in one direction and Bill in another. I was very upset and felt the need to find a quiet place to pray. God brought to mind that our battle is not with flesh and blood, but with principalities and powers of this dark age.

For we wrestle not against flesh and blood, but against principalities, against powers, against the rulers of the darkness of this world, against spiritual wickedness in high places. (Ephesians 6:12 KJV)

I felt God telling me to find Bill and deal with the problem. Bill had also gone off to pray with the same result. It ended up with both of us asking each other's forgiveness and then praying together. During the entire time we worked together, we never had another situation like this again.

About this time the auction company's secretary experienced a marriage breakup. We had a shared experience of our partners leaving us, so we naturally were drawn to each other. At times, I worried we were becoming too close, so I prayed that God would place a barrier between us. It felt as though a pane of glass separated us, we could see and talk to each other, but could not get close. I told God that I thought His barrier was a bit too effective. However, I am pleased to say that we have remained firm friends over the years and she became like a sister to me.

I had prayed that my son-in-law David, who was unemployed at the time, would find a job working with Christians. In the meantime, I had managed to get him some casual work helping with auctions and cartage jobs that I had been doing. One day, as I was driving back from an auction, I sensed God laughing. When I asked why, He said, "So you wanted David to work for Christians?" This playful teasing helped me deepen my relationship with God. During the many hours I spent driving, I enjoyed listening to worship music, and I appreciated the quiet moments of enjoying His presence.

During the legal separation between Carol and I, our lawyers were working out the details. I tried to handle the process biblically, seeking guidance from the elders of our church, but it proved quite difficult as it involved the subdivision of our shared property. At one point, I felt that God was not speaking to me, so I turned to my mentors for advice. The mentor's wife asked me probing questions and then pointedly asked, "Do you want God to write it in the sky for you?" It turned out that God had been communicating with me, but I had failed to hear it.

The subdivision of the property did not align with the local council's guidelines, yet permission to subdivide was granted in just three weeks. In contrast, another Christian organisation in the same county required many months to obtain approval for a legal subdivision in their case.

Carol had always regularly attended church and she had bought me a lovely Bible that I did want to read, but it was always over on her side of the bed. Wanting to have my own copy, I decided to buy the cheapest Bible I could, and found one that promised a programme to "read the Bible in a year." When I got it home, I could not locate the programme in the index, leaving me unsure of what to read. Then one night, I heard God say, "Read it every day." As I picked up the Bible, it fell open to the exact page where the programme notes were. Since then, I have made a conscientious effort to commit to my daily Bible reading.

Thankfulness

While I was driving on the motorway from Papakura to Auckland one day, I felt God wanted to give me a special gift. I was crossing the Papakura causeway at the time; the tide was in and the water sparkling and it was very calm. He said that was His special gift to me. Ever since, when I drive over that piece of road I am reminded of His gracious offering. Sometimes it is stormy and sometimes the tide is out, but is still very special to me.

Before 1990, while I had always enjoyed pretty views, they became so much more vibrant once I realised that they were God's gifts, not only for me, but also to any who wanted to see them as God's creation.

As I have travelled the world, I have encountered many remarkable sights that have drawn my attention to God's gifts. For instance, while I was working in Hong Kong, I admired the scenic drive up the coast from Tuen Mun to Pillar Point. Another special sight was the tiny flowers miraculously growing out of cracks in the concrete, at the refugee camp.

Beyond these examples, I've marvelled at: the tremendous colour and vibrancy of the flowers in the north of England during their short season; the power and majesty of the North Sea at South Shields in the United Kingdom; the Tasman Sea on the coast at Mōkau, and the Southern Alps rising up from the Canterbury Plains in New Zealand; the birds in the trees, green grass of paddocks, animals grazing, the scent of the different flowers and I could go on…

FOUR

MERCY MISSIONS

In December 1990 full-time missionaries Rex and Barbara Stone appeared at First Church. They had been away at Rise Up – an approach to unite all the churches in New Zealand. They were on furlough and were planning to go away again in the New Year with a follow-up programme called Team Missions. I immediately prayed and asked God whether I could be a part of that programme, but in His usual wisdom He maintained His silence, so I regretfully felt that I was not to go.

Rex and Barb became very good friends of mine. Rex was previously an alcoholic who had been violent towards his family. Initially, God used a friend that did not normally attend church, but whose wife did, to take Rex to church. With the encouragement of the pastor and Barb, Rex continued attending. During this time, a compassionate minister helped Rex's family discover God's love and healing, which restored their self-worth. God then prepared Rex and Barb for a special ministry of their own. They completed Discipleship Training School with their church and then went on to attend Lifeway Bible College north of Auckland.

Rex and Barb did not go away to Team Missions, the sequel to Rise Up, as God had other plans for them. Although they had already arranged to rent out their flat, they felt that they were to stay in Papakura and start a ministry to serve the local poor. The flat unexpectedly became available, so they called for volunteers and started an organisation called Mercy Missions.

The first donations they received were from local farmers – potatoes and flowers. They asked God for guidance and felt led to distribute them to individuals in Papakura. So they and their volunteers drove through the streets asking God which households to give them to. As they went, they also asked if the people had any needs, physical or spiritual. They helped elderly resident with their gardens and lawns, and helped the sick and disabled. Mercy Missions soon developed into a Christian Food Bank with more importance being put on spiritual food than physical food. One of the houses that they called at, while giving away the flowers and potatoes, belonged to a senior manager in the local Dairy Company, who then arranged for a large donation of yoghurt to be given to those in need.

Despite my fervent prayers, God did not direct me to join Mercy Missions at this time. I did offer the services of my truck to transport food or firewood if I was available. After six months, they began to occasionally utilise my services. Although I was still not directed by God to join them, my truck and I were used increasingly over the course of the year.

At 10 am one morning, we were offered 34 tonnes of soft drinks, but we had to pick them up before 2 pm! Barb quickly arranged for three extra trucks, and I was required to collect three loads. Rex asked me to take his grandson, Matthew, with me. As we had not had lunch, I stopped to get some, and discovered that I had left my wallet at home. I did not have enough money to buy two lunches, so decided to just get one for Matthew. When I went into the lunch bar, the cashier unexpectedly offered me all the remaining food in the cabinet for the small amount of cash I had. There was more than enough to feed both of us and the other drivers. I was amazed by this act of generosity, which taught me an important lesson about faith. I used to have trouble accepting help from others, until someone pointed out that if I didn't allow it, I would be preventing God from assisting me.

In early December, we faced a food shortage, believing we only had enough for ten families, despite needing more. Upstairs in the flat, we prayed to God, recalling Christ's miracles of feeding the 5,000 and 4,000 people (Matthew 14-15), and asking Him to perform a modern-day miracle. To our surprise, we were able to deliver over 40 food parcels that day, with ten more left over. From that point on, we never experienced a food shortage again, even as the number of families we fed grew to over 1,400.

Early in the following year, I attended a Christian conference called "Breakout," where many leaders from all over the world came to speak to us. At that conference I felt God calling me to work with Mercy Missions full-time. I didn't want to step out in my own strength, so like Gideon (Judges 6:33-40), I "cast a fleece" to confirm that I had heard God correctly. I asked for two confirmations. The first came from Bruce Benge, who was assistant pastor at the church that I was attending, and the second came from my cousin Bill, who stated that when I had delivered some food from Mercy Missions to their area before Christmas, that I was in my element. So I commenced working with them full-time.

Right from the start I was kept busy picking up truckloads of food and supplies, helping to cut and cart firewood to give away. We prayed together most days for our needs, and giving thanks to God for our provision. We also prayed for the needs of others and our local churches.

One of the special things that happened at Mercy Missions was that the team prayed together each day, and on three days of the week we had a time of Praise and Worship. I found that the more time that I spent doing these things, the closer I got to God and the more He seemed to speak with me. I also made it my priority to read the Bible every day and spend time with God so that I would have a deeper relationship with Him.

Mercy Missions provided ongoing spiritual training for all their staff, though I initially failed to appreciate the value of these sessions. Much later while overseas, I was to discover the true value of their ideas.

Rex and Barb handled the food distribution and storage from their flat, which soon left no room for their own car in the garage as it became filled with the growing stockpile of food. Occasionally, the surplus would need to be stored outside, much to the annoyance of their neighbours in the apartment block. This frustration only intensified when the volunteers and their vehicles arrived to collect and deliver the food parcels, completely blocking the driveway as people loaded up.

It soon became apparent that Mercy Missions would need to relocate. The Mercy Missions organisation itself had no money, as their policy was to have as little involvement with it as possible. We all prayed about it and looked at several properties and warehouses that we might have been able to get for free, but none of them were suitable. So, back to the prayer board.

One day, we learned of a property that had once been an orchard, but the previous owner had cut down all the trees. The property included a large shed and a nice house, which the current owner was renting out while waiting to sell the entire property. We tried to rent the house and sheds, but the deal never materialised. Eventually, we felt that God was calling us to purchase the property, but we faced a significant obstacle – the $320,000 price tag and a lack of available funds. We were unsure of how to proceed.

A $100 donation was made towards the property purchase, and Rex and Barb were prepared to contribute the value of their flat. However, this would only amount to one-sixth of the total property value. After much prayer by those involved, it was decided to purchase the property outright through faith. The agreement required a $20,000 deposit to move in, with certain sums needing to be met by fixed dates or the mission would be evicted, and all previous payments would be forfeited. Once half the property value was reached, that eviction clause would no longer be valid.

At one point, Mercy Missions did not have enough funds to make a required payment. Rex approached me and asked if I could help. I agreed to pray about it, and ultimately felt that God did not want me to provide financial assistance. When I relayed this to Rex, he was disappointed and persistently begged me to reconsider. Against my initial instincts, I ended up loaning Mercy Missions $13,000.

A few days later, a church contacted Rex and inquired about the remaining amount needed to complete the next payment. Rex informed them it was $7,000, and the church stated they had been prepared to give up to $20,000 to finish the deal. This unexpected contribution was a positive outcome and a valuable lesson for all involved.

Around the time I departed Mercy Missions, the organisation had reached the halfway point in raising the necessary funds for the property.

In the early days, Mercy Missions, like many faith-living organisations, was often short of materials to do various jobs. I remember that several times we were short of nails and staples for the many jobs that we wanted to do. As the mission had no money, the only option was to turn to prayer. For a long time we got just enough to do the job in hand. One day, a car pulled into the mission's gates, and the driver offered us boxes upon boxes of nails – the very supplies we had been lacking. It turned out the driver worked for a nail manufacturing company and was offering the "sweepings" from the factory floor, a mix of sizes that was not economical for the company to sort. This generous donation provided the mission with ample nails that served our needs for many years to come.

While I was still working with Mercy Missions, I was asked to join a Discipleship training course called Troops in Training (TNT) put on by First Church. I was initially hesitant to be involved, but after much encouragement from God, Rex, and Barb, I finally agreed. I had thought I could continue driving the truck to collect food and fit the course around that, but in reality, I had to devote my full attention to the intensive three-month programme.

The course ran Tuesday through to Friday, with lectures and ministry every morning and practical Christianity activities in the afternoons. These included delivering food parcels, gardening and tidying around the church, drain digging, catering for functions, and visiting hospital patients and other churches. Our lecturers were drawn from several Bible colleges in the upper North Island, as well as from YWAM (Youth with a Mission) and those who had served as missionaries and pastors. The curriculum covered a wide range of topics and was very intensive. We also took turns leading worship and preaching at various churches throughout the course.

In addition to the TNT programme, I participated in numerous other training courses, such as "Walls of Your Heart" by Dr Bruce Thompson, which were designed for YWAM. These courses have been invaluable in strengthening my Christian faith and journey.

One day while we were delivering parcels during TNT, we were sent to a non-existent address. As we searched nearby houses, we came across a distressed lady at the final house. After she had told us that this was not the address we were after, she told us that she had no food for her children and could only give them black tea to try to ease their hunger. Recognising this was a needy case, we gave her the food parcels.

Checking back at Mercy Missions, we confirmed the address we had been given was correct and had been properly phoned in. We concluded that God had purposefully directed us to this woman in need, who had been praying for assistance.

While visiting another home, we found a distressed mother holding her ill baby. We asked if we could pray for the baby and the mother readily agreed, admitting she was not Christian herself. We proceeded to pray for both the baby and the mother. When we returned to the home sometime later, the mother joyfully informed us that the baby had been miraculously healed

After completing the discipleship school training, we were sent on an outreach trip to the tropical islands of Vanuatu in the South Pacific. We were ferried across to a tiny island at the mouth of Port Vila harbour in a small open boat, as there were no vehicles or roads on this particular island – only well-kept paths. One of our tasks was to spread fresh shells on the paths and trim back the encroaching foliage.

Our worship team was rather taken aback at the first service that we attended, as the local Presbyterian church did not believe in having instruments to sing along with. They finally allowed us to use one guitar to lead our singing. Later we were invited to another church that welcomed our instruments. I later came to the conclusion that when the first missionaries had arrived it would have been very difficult to have transported a piano ashore, so a tradition had been born to worship without musical instruments.

During this mission trip to Vanuatu, I was asked to preach at a local church. Initially, my sermon did not flow well. However, as I continued, the message came together, and the service went quite smoothly. Afterward, two women approached me and shared that they had sensed someone in the congregation praying against me. They discerned this person's identity, sat on either side of them, and prayed silently in tongues. The individual then got up and left. From that point on, my preaching flowed effortlessly.

The island had a traditional practice where the women were solely responsible for washing up, and they did not appreciate the men's help. One night, I felt compelled to assist with the chores despite the women's protests. As we worked together, I shared a bit of my personal testimony, which led to an invitation to speak at an Assembly of God house group. With my leader's approval, I gathered a team, and we had a wonderful evening of sharing with the group. Encouraged by this, we were then invited to preach at their church the following Sunday, which we did.

However, during our time there, we discovered a significant miscalculation in the funds needed for our stay. We agreed to pool all the money we had, including what we had brought to buy gifts for our loved ones back home. One couple was unwilling to contribute their funds, but we managed to have just enough to meet our commitments. As we were leaving, the islanders generously gave us gifts far better than what we could have purchased ourselves. Interestingly, the couple who had refused to pool their funds did not receive any gifts from the islanders. Our enjoyable two-week stay in Vanuatu came to an end.

At times, you may be given a prophecy that seems so improbable as to be almost laughable. Yet, you are in esteemed company, with many biblical stories that seem impossible at first, but were later proven true. When I was fifty-four, I was given such a prophecy – that I would have many sons and daughters. This seemed far-fetched, as my wife had left me and we only had three daughters.

However, the prophecy did come to pass, in the remarkable way only God can manage. The first came at a Christian conference, where a young woman asked me to be her spiritual father, as she lacked a paternal figure. Soon after, a young man at the same conference requested that I be his spiritual dad as well. This pattern continued wherever my ministry took me – I gained many spiritual sons and daughters around the world.

During the first Mercy Missions retreat held in my woolshed, a 12-year-old boy provided me with a verse which remains one of my favourites:

Trust in the Lord with all your heart,
And lean not on your own understanding;
In all your ways acknowledge Him,
And He shall direct your paths.
(Proverbs 3:5-6)

In February 1994 I decided to take on the role of Resource Manager for Mercy Missions, a job that involved canvassing for food and supplies. This decision came after much thought and prayer, as I did not feel I had the necessary qualifications. However, with encouragement from others and the availability of someone to handle the truck driving, I decided to give it a try.

I committed to do this job for the next six months, as I felt it was important to have continuity in this role. Before approaching any supplier, I would often gather others to pray with me. Many times the companies would tell me it was a waste of time to come and visit them. On nearly every occasion I would walk out of the offices leaving behind a person with a puzzled look on their face, thinking, "Why did I give so much to that mission?" I believe God went before me, and His provision proved to be enormous. Through faith and perseverance, I was able to secure the resources needed to support the important work of Mercy Missions.

While working with Mercy Missions, we were all delighted to see Rex and Barb receive a local newspaper award for their community service. Rex and I could almost pass as brothers as we have similar looks and friends have commented we look alike. The day the article was published, I stopped in a shop to buy groceries. To my surprise, a woman approached me, congratulating me on the wonderful work my wife and I were doing. I explained that I was not Rex, but the woman refused to believe me, insisting I was just being modest. Despite my protests, she remained convinced I was the award recipient, and there was no way I could convince her otherwise.

After my six-month commitment, I informed Rex of my plan to leave Mercy Missions. Initially, he reacted with distress, questioning whether I had truly heard God's direction. However, later that day, he approached me to apologise, explaining that his concern stemmed from finding a suitable replacement. We then prayed together, and he released me to follow wherever God was leading.

The *Anastasis* Mercy Ship had visited New Zealand in the early eighties, while it was serving in the Pacific after travelling from its rebuild in Greece. Seeking potential volunteers, they advertised that visitors could come on board and take a look. I decided that it looked interesting, so at the time, I took a trip into Auckland and toured the ship. It also travelled to New Plymouth while on a 14-port tour of the country, and I later saw it there. Seeing the ship's operation at the time kindled my interest, and I had filed this away as a mental note and maybe "potential future task" list.

God's Protection and Provision

Near my home is a winding road, and I often pray for safety as I drive it – "God, keep me and others safe." On several occasions, I've been grateful for that protection. And I still pray this prayer today.

One day after a long auction setup, I was driving home exhausted. As I accelerated, a truck towing an unlighted trailer pulled out in front of me. The trailer was nearly invisible, and I had to brake hard to avoid a collision. At the time, I would have been travelling at 80 km/hr and thought there was no way I could stop, but to my amazement, I pulled up in time. I couldn't believe how close I had come to a dangerous accident, and I was deeply thankful for the divine intervention that kept me safe.

One night, after attending a house group, I was driving up through a gorge when I encountered a car speeding down the hill on my side of the road. The driver's speed was too high for him to safely return to his own lane. I didn't dare swerve onto the other side, as that would have caused a collision if the other driver had managed to regain control. Somehow, the other car was able to squeeze past me on the wrong side of the road. I was grateful to God for His protection during many similar close calls.

A friend called me one time, desperate because he had run out of water. He relied on rainwater, and both his tanks were empty. He asked if he could use some funds that were under his control, but not technically his own, even though they would become his in two weeks. I advised him not to use the money until it was legally his, though I felt sheepish about this. He asked me what he should do, as he had no money of his own. It was Friday night, and he lived a considerable distance away. I suggested he and his wife turn on their taps and pray until the water started flowing. They did so, and after three-quarters of an hour, the water began running and continued all weekend, stopping on Monday morning at 9 am. Just 30 minutes later, a truck arrived with a water delivery donated by someone.

Sometime later I called on my friend and he was in one of those spiritually dry places that most of us seem to reach occasionally, and I asked him if he had been praising the Lord and giving Him thanks. He felt that there was nothing to give thanks for! I reminded him about the water and he fell to his knees and asked God's forgiveness. It showed me how easy it is to forget God's miracles, like the Israelites in the desert.

While assisting with a show put on by our local theatre group, a drunk man insisted on interrupting the show to publicly declare his intent to stop drinking alcohol. Aware that there was a warrant out for his arrest, the local pastor contacted the authorities. "Mac" managed to escape before the police arrived, but was later apprehended and detained until he had sobered up. The pastor discovered that Mac had been evicted from his home by his wife, who could no longer tolerate his alcoholism, and he asked me whether I could give Mac a home for a few nights.

The arrest warrants had somehow been misplaced, so he was released from custody the next morning. I collected him from the church office, and told him he could stay with me but only if he did not bring any alcohol into the house – which he agreed to. He brought with him a fairly heavy overnight bag. During his stay, I offered to pray with him at any hour of the day or night, to help him overcome his problems. That evening before bed, we decided to have a prayer time. As I prayed, I invited the Holy Spirit to take control, and to help him through the night. Suddenly, as we were praying, he jumped up and rushed to pour all the booze from his overnight bag down our kitchen sink. Realising he might find the drinks cabinet in my house, I waited until he fell asleep, then moved the alcohol into a locked shed to prevent undoing the work of the Holy Spirit.

During the initial three months, Mac frequently called on me, day or night, to pray with him. It was encouraging to see Mac become independent from alcohol. He accompanied me to work daily at Mercy Missions, where I or another staff member was always available to assist him. Eventually he was reconciled with his wife and returned home. One evening I was invited to dinner at their place, and during the meal the wife and daughter appeared very teary. When I asked what was wrong, they told me that I was the first guest that had a meal with them in the last ten years, where Mac was sober.

Despite Mac's initial success in overcoming his addiction, his recovery was short-lived. One day a couple of non-Christian relief drivers thought it would be a "joke" to offer Mac a drink which sadly led him back into the grip of alcoholism. At the time, I didn't realise it, but this experience proved to be valuable training for me in learning how to deal with the complications of addiction.

When I spent extended time in worship, God would often reveal to me someone who was deeply hurting, and I often felt prompted to approach them to see if I could help. One person initially was in denial, but I persisted in prayer. Months later, the person admitted I had been right all along. Many times, as I prayed for individuals, ideas would come to mind to share with them. Sharing these thoughts often revealed an area requiring prayer, which I otherwise would not have known.

Call to Hong Kong

After I had indicated to Rex my time at Mercy Missions was ending, my mentors suggested several places that needed missionaries, so I started to pray for guidance about them. The two choices that it boiled down to were: St Stephen's Society in Hong Kong; and YWAM Harpenden in England. St Stephen's Society is a missionary organisation, devoted to rehabilitation and healing drug addicts, and looking after the Vietnamese refugees. I felt that this work of Jackie Pullinger's with the drug addicts in Hong Kong was the most likely place I would begin my full-time overseas mission work.

On the day that I got my legal separation papers from the lawyer, I also got an invitation to work in Hong Kong, quickly followed the next day by an invitation to work for YWAM at Harpenden, England. I felt that as the invitation to Hong Kong had arrived on the day the legal papers had arrived, that this was God giving me a sign where to go first.

When I heard God's call to go to Hong Kong, I felt it was

important that a replacement Resource Manager be found before I departed. I left Mercy Mission six months to the day, and God indeed provided the person to take over the role.

After making the decision, it was absolutely amazing how many other things fell into place. I sold my van, and rented out my house. In the last few days, I also purchased a rental flat, which, combined with the house rent, would provide the financial independence that I needed for my time as a missionary.

As part of my preparations to go to Hong Kong I went to have a medical check-up and discovered that my blood pressure was dangerously high. The doctor told me that I would be unable to leave until I had it under control. Immediately he put me on medication, and prescribed walking as a way of helping to lower it. As I had felt well, and very fit, it was quite a shock. I feel that it was another of God's blessings to discover it before anything else happened.

Although I love aviation, I have never enjoyed navigating airports on my own. Initially I had planned to travel over to Hong Kong with another Christian woman who was also due to start at St Stephen's, but her circumstances changed and she could no longer join me. As a result I was quite apprehensive heading away by myself.

FIVE

HONG KONG

Fear not, for I am with you;
Be not dismayed, for I am your God.
I will strengthen you,
Yes, I will help you,
I will uphold you with My righteous right hand.
(Isaiah 41:10)

I arrived in Hong Kong on September 10, 1994, to work with the St Stephen's Society in Kowloon. At that time, the old airport at Hong Kong was still in operation. It was once considered among the most remarkable airport landings in the world. A pilot friend once told me it was one of the most challenging places he had ever landed. On descent towards the airstrip, high-rise buildings surrounded the plane, and on occasion, you could clearly see families eating their dinner! This was especially spectacular at night.

Coming from a quiet farm and cool spring temperatures in New Zealand, I found Hong Kong very hot, noisy, and extremely crowded. I met up with a team of Canadians from Langley Vineyard Church, and we had a one-week orientation course together. We were all accommodated in a former army camp called Hang Fook Camp in Kowloon.

> *In 1985 Hong Kong Government offered us Hang Fook Camp in urban Kowloon, a disused tin hut area (THA) where many people of all kinds, including the poor and elderly, gathered to worship and eat with us. We began training all of them to heal the sick and share their food with the hungry. It became famous as a place for Christmas feasts, miracles and sodden, baking hot meetings!*[1]

The buildings were single-storey tin shacks, with rooms measuring either 9 feet by 8 feet or twice that size. There was a communal dining area, which was also used for the Church services. Up to 150 people could be in residence at any time. On the second day of the orientation course, Jackie Pullinger came rushing into the room where we were, saying that the United Nations had just given us a Refugee Camp at Pillar Point to operate. The United Nations (UN) office in Hong Kong was led by a predominantly Muslim administration, making it all the more remarkable that they asked a Christian organisation to undertake this task. This unexpected request was nothing short of a miracle.

> *After visiting Hang Fook Camp in 1994 UNHCR officials invited St Stephen's Society to manage and run a Vietnamese Refugee Camp for them. It was the last remaining camp – only a few thousand people were left. We saw many drug-free and resettled before the refugee crisis was over and the UN withdrew from HK.*[2]

As part of our training we were sent out to deliver Rice Boxes to homeless people (street sleepers). It was quite a shock to see so many homeless sleeping in shop doorways, or on park benches. The conditions here are nothing like you will ever see in New Zealand, and many visitors describe their shock at seeing the conditions. In the cold weather, the St Stephen's Society would deliver blankets to them as well. These blankets had been given to St Stephen's by one of the major hotels as they had marks on them and couldn't be used for their clients. There is no welfare assistance available to the homeless in Hong Kong. After we had finished the course we were sent out to the "New Boy Houses" to help the boys to come off drugs (mostly heroin), and start a new life. The "House" concept came about from Jackie's early experiences where drug addicts had come to stay with her, and upon praying and giving their lives to Jesus, their addictions were easily overcome.

> *That's how our "houses" started in the seventies and have continued in the same way, with the same wonderful miracle of painless withdrawal from drugs as we pray in the Spirit. We did not advertise but by word of mouth, one man in prison told another, "You can go to Jackie's (Poon's place) and start a new life." Hardly a street sleeper who had not heard, 'There is a place you can go to... More and more overseas helpers joined the adventure. Former addicts got jobs and helped in their spare time, some working full time with us. We started homes for teenagers, English speaking addicts, then women and girls. Over the years, we've borrowed or rented over 287 places to house the poor, recovering addicts and those with life-threatening problems. Some of these were given on a temporary basis by the Hong Kong Government and several in outlying areas.*[3]

New Boy House

I was sent to B11 – a house at Tai Po led by Hayley Graham, a very capable young lady from England who was quite fluent in Cantonese. She was just re-starting the house as the previous intake of boys had moved on to the second stage house. The night that I arrived, one of the Chinese helpers had just been bitten by a snake, and no one had any idea whether it was poisonous or not. Several people prayed for him and by the next day he was all right. I spent quite a lot of time discovering myself, and learning to rely more on God.

These houses had been former police holiday homes. They accommodated up to forty addicts. There was a kitchen, dining room, several bathrooms and toilets, and four bunk rooms, sleeping approximately ten people. There was an office for the leader, and a passage joining all the rooms together. All the outside windows and doors were barred and they were all locked at night. The main objective was to stop the addicts running away. Our accommodation often suffered from the tropical conditions – during rainstorms we had up to six buckets on the floor catching drips from the leaking ceilings. Later we managed to repair the roof so less buckets were needed. The washing up was done at an outside bench with cold water. Outside there was a terrace where the addicts could sit after their ten-day withdrawal period when the helpers had time to sit with them.

There were six houses in total within 100 metres of each other: four houses for the men – three for drug addicts and one for alcoholics; two houses for the women addicts, and helpers. A large area for sports was near the women's houses, where extremely competitive games of volleyball were played.

As the Hong Kong climate is tropical and wet, there is vigorous plant growth which meant an everlasting job to keep it in check. Both the addicts and the helpers had to help. There was a wonderful view from the boys' houses, where we could see the sea, and a large water dam for fresh water in an area that had been reclaimed from the sea.

We took in "New Boys" for rehabilitation two at a time. A roster was set up, and for the first ten to twelve days they were never on their own. At least one of the helpers was with them all the time, even when they went to the toilet or had a shower, in case they had managed to get hold of some drugs. We prayed with them, or for them, 24 hours a day. For the first ten days, the boys were only allowed to wear pyjamas, their own clothes having been taken away from them and locked away. At full capacity there were 27 addicts and six staff.

During the nights we worked in pairs in four-hour shifts. I was quite frustrated that I could not speak to them as they did not appear to understand English, but I kept asking God to help me to learn their language. One day He said quite clearly to me that I did not need words to show His love for them! So I learnt that verbal conversation was not totally necessary. It was wonderful to see God at work taking the boys through withdrawal from drugs, without the usual pain and suffering, as soon as they were prepared to give their hearts totally to Him. It also seemed to help if they could pray in tongues (God's own special language that He grants us for prayer). Later I saw the terrible withdrawal pains that some of the addicts went through when they would not accept God's help. Language does not matter in worship, and communication can be non-verbal.

We shared the rooms with the addicts. There were usually about ten of us sharing each room, but if it was full there could be many more, and it was often very noisy during the night with people getting up or going back to bed. This would go on all night as the addicts were often very restless and unable to sleep. When I was not on duty, one of the things that helped me to sleep was to put on a quiet worship tape and set my cassette tape player onto continuous play using the head phones, so it didn't disturb the others around me.

On one occasion I felt the need to write to Papakura East Presbyterian Church in New Zealand about one of the boys, and asked them to pray for him. The day that they received the letter he ran away from the house. The church, not knowing this, started to pray for him. The day that I received the reply from the pastor, saying that they were praying for him, the boy walked back into the house asking to be re-admitted. He was very touched that a church in far away New Zealand was praying for him, and I am pleased to report that two years later he is still with the St Stephen's Society helping others to come off drugs.

There were 12 boys in the house and many actually could understand or speak English but didn't want us to know. On one occasion we were having a quiet time with the boys, and God told me that one of them spoke English, so I said to him, "You speak English, don't you?" He replied, "Who told you?" I answered, "God." He looked as surprised as I felt. He became a good friend of mine. After God revealed this to me, I found out that most of them spoke or at least understood English. This boy later showed me how to read the grocery pricing at the markets, which became invaluable.

In Hong Kong there are markets for Westerners and locals, and the "local" markets had significantly lower prices. I would go and listen to the locals haggling, and then I would step in and ask the price for items I wanted to buy. Initially they gave me the Westerners' price, but from my knowledge gained from the boys I became skilled at my vegetable negotiation.

While out and about, I was always amazed to see new high-rise buildings under construction. The workers used rickety bamboo scaffolding, along which motorised wheelbarrows loaded with concrete rattled precariously. The entire setup looked so hazardous that I was surprised there were not more accidents and spills!

I encountered a 70-year-old lady carrying a huge heap of cardboard on her head. I later discovered that this was her means of earning a living. She was living in a little shelter on her own and had found faith in Christ after years of being a prostitute. Without fail, she attended our Sunday services at the camp.

I was told about a time when some of the Western helpers from the New Boy houses were returning from an outing, and as they neared home, they noticed an old man walking along the road in his pyjamas. Mistaking him for a runaway "New Boy," they captured him, and carried him, struggling violently, back to the house. After they got there, they discovered that they had captured one of the regular villagers who had been going about his daily business! This incident caused us to become unpopular with the locals.

One special time for me was attending the baptism of some of the brothers who had given their hearts to Jesus. This was held in a public park, and there were several hundred people from the St Stephen's Society. Many people shared their testimony, and we had a time of worship which was relayed through a sound system. Quite a number of the other people in the park became very interested, and our people spent some time counselling and talking to them about Jesus.

During my work at the New Boy House, I was introduced to a practice that I found very helpful. We were asked to take an afternoon and go to some place of our own choosing, to spend that time with God. At first I found it quite difficult, but as I persevered it became a very important time for me. We were allowed to bring our Bible, and perhaps some worship music.

The first time I climbed up on a high hill and for most of the afternoon I was distracted by the views, boats on the water, and activity going on down below. But as I persisted in pressing into God, He gradually began to reveal Himself to me. From my recollection of that first afternoon, I probably only spent half an hour in His presence. God started to point out things about His creation, leaving me with a desire to know Him better. Pressing into God is a term used to indicate communing with God through Bible reading and prayer.

Another time, He guided me to have that time in a bare room in a house, with only a table and a chair in the room. For a short while I wondered why He had asked me to have this time there. Then He asked me to write down all the things in that room that were of His creation. For a start it was quite difficult, but as he opened my eyes, I saw so many things, and wrote down over two hundred. That afternoon passed very quickly as I admired His handiwork in the apparently bare space.

The next occasion, I felt drawn to spend time under the busiest flyover at Yau Ma Tei. There was a tiny garden there with a hard wooden seat. At first I sat on the seat, and all I could hear was the rush of vehicles above. There was a continuous noise of rumbling double-decker buses, the roar of the trucks as they pulled away from the traffic lights, and a constant hum of voices as thousands walked past just a few feet away.

As I sat there on my uncomfortable seat, I saw a tiny, beautiful butterfly fly past. This drew my attention to the lush vegetation and reminded me of the beauty of the plants that grew at my home in New Zealand. Then the noise and clamour around faded away and I could hear several different small birds singing.

The fine and warm afternoon suddenly turned cold and wet, making my seat grow increasingly uncomfortable. I had to abandon my post and head to the nearest McDonalds to buy a hot drink to warm myself up. God called my attention to the fact that if I had been a street sleeper, I would have nowhere to go and would have been unable to have afford a warm drink. As I sipped my drink, I noticed some exceptionally well-dressed schoolgirls wearing very expensive gold jewellery. Later when I returned to Hang Fook Camp, I asked about these girls, where one of the leaders informed me that they were schoolgirl prostitutes. I realise that I was quite naive back then.

...make every effort to enter [Gods'] rest... (Hebrews 4:11 NIV)

I continue to enjoy these quiet times with God, and would encourage others to press in to Him in this manner.

God's Provision

One day I broke my camera, and when I took it to a repair shop, they told me it was not repairable. Since it was not a necessity, I felt I could do without one. A short time later my church blessed me with a donation of cash for Christmas. After praying, I decided I would buy a new camera, but firstly I paid a tithe out of the amount, and then went to look at cameras. I found a camera I liked, and to my delight, the remaining amount was exactly what I needed to buy the camera and a roll of film – there was no leftover change!

At the New Boy Houses, we were required to do night duties

two nights a week. This involved a lot of travelling all around Hong Kong as we worked in all the different houses. One night, two of the girls and I were walking to one of the New Boy houses when we saw a tiny dead snake lying on the road. One of the girls became quite scared and upset. I remembered a Christian "combat" song that I had learnt in New Zealand, where we have no snakes. The song was based on the following verse:

> *I have given you authority to walk on snakes and scorpions and crush them under your feet.* (Adapted from Luke 10:19)

After learning this scripture, one night while walking home, she stepped on a large snake in the dark. She claimed God's words and came to no harm.

Hang Fook Camp

After working in the New Boy Houses for three weeks, we were recalled to Hang Fook Camp to go "prayer walking." We were sent to pray around the United Nations building, in the hope they would release a property for the Vietnamese addict work. I was very sad to leave the New Boy House. The management of St Stephen's asked me to lead a team of young Canadians on the prayer walking outside the camp as there were no other leaders available at the time. This was an unofficial leadership role and management were relying on my age to lend authority. The Canadians were unaware of my leadership role, which made it challenging at times, as I felt I lacked the proper authority to effectively carry out my responsibilities.

We spent a lot of time praying through the Pillar Point Refugee camp that St Stephen's Society was hoping to run. The first time that I went into the camp, I felt all the hairs on the back of my neck stand up. In fact, I was quite apprehensive on entering the camp because of the unseen spiritual forces there. Anyway, we spent many evenings as a team praying though the camp. Some time later, one of the St Stephen's Society leaders came to Pillar Point to speak at the drug addicts meeting, and as we were leaving the camp he remarked that it had changed. I asked why and he said that the first time that he had entered the camp he had the same experience of the hairs on the back of his neck standing up, but now all he felt was the peace that was there.

When I had been leading the prayer teams through the camp, I did not have much faith in the prayers that I had been offering to God, and He chose that testimony to change my heart.

The Canadians and I were also involved in extensive prayer, walking around various places considered important to the Vietnamese programme. The sites included the United Nations Building at Yau Ma Tei, the District Council Offices at Yuen Long, Pillar Point and a camp at Pak Nai.

The refugee camp at Pak Nai, under the control of the army, was closely guarded by a security firm, and several times we tried to gain entry without success. I spent some time praying that God would open doors for us. Then one day, when Jody Farmer and I were praying around Pak Nai, the guard came out and invited us in to see the camp. I had felt that God was going to give it to us for the Vietnamese work, but it never came about.

While I was living at Hang Fook, I was often asked to do some driving, and this usually involved driving all around Hong Kong. As I was not familiar with the streets, they often sent the former drug addicts with me to show me the way. This was quite hazardous as they often had no experience of driving themselves, and tended to tell you to exit now, especially when you were driving in one of the middle lanes of an eight-lane highway. If we missed that exit we were often hopelessly lost. Some of them had a charming habit of directing us through "Bus Only" streets, or down "One Way" streets the wrong way. Many of the drivers had occasion to rue their directions. On one occasion my guides directed me down a bus only street, which I had not noticed, and I was pulled up by a policeman who gave me a tongue lashing, fortunately I did not get a ticket. I think it was because the boys were grinning so broadly that he took pity on me.

Another time my guides had even less idea of where we were supposed to be going, and we got hopelessly lost, driving around for ages until I finally spotted a road that I knew, then we managed to find our way back to camp. The next morning the brothers started to tease me about getting lost, so I introduced them to my "Tour Directors," and from then on I had little problems with my guides. Later, I came to realise that as the drug addicts had only ever walked everywhere, Bus Only and one-way streets would have little meaning to them. I hope that they have forgiven me for thinking that they did it deliberately.

Living at Hang Fook meant that you were required to be involved in the camp programmes. This meant helping to take the Rice Boxes out to the street sleepers or attending the drug addicts meetings. These were people who had no home to go to, so they would set up house on the footpath, putting a piece of cardboard down to sleep on. In some cases they made little cardboard houses under one of the many highway flyovers, or in an alley. Most of these people had no choice of where to live as there is no welfare assistance in Hong Kong.

During a church service at Hang Fook Camp, someone received a divine message to pray around the coastlines of Hong

Kong and the New Territories. The purpose of these prayers was to seek forgiveness for the wrongs committed by foreign powers that had entered and occupied the region in the past. Our group decided that we would go to Sai Kung to pray along that coastline. Everyone was to meet at McDonalds at 2 pm on Saturday, and as I had never been there before, I was unable to get there on time. Following directions, I eventually managed to find the McDonalds store, but had no idea where to find our group. I asked God how to find them, and as I walked, I felt suggestions being put into my mind, "turn this way" or "go straight" and I soon met up with part of the group who were absolute strangers to me.

Afterwards we met together at a local person's house for a debriefing and a shared meal. There, I met a guy whose wife had recently left him. We became firm friends, and often prayed together. Much later he told me about a group from another church who had been praying for him. As he had listened to their prayers, he had been amazed at the personal knowledge that they knew about him, which affected him very deeply. Later he asked them how they knew all the issues to pray about. And it turned out that they had been praying in tongues, but he had heard them in English!

One day we were asked to go up on a small mountain in the buffer zone between Hong Kong and China, to pray over China before a team from St Stephen's Society went out to pray over the ground of Chairman Mao's Long March. There had been several of these teams who eventually covered all the ground of that march, in prayer. On that day quite a number of people were praying on the mountain for the team, and several had prophecies for the team.

As we came down the mountain, one of the men who had

given a prophecy, started looking very unwell. I asked him if he was alright, and he replied that he had a terrible pain in his chest and left arm. His face was all blotchy, and as he looked decidedly unwell, I thought he could be having a heart attack. I gathered three others to pray for him. As we prayed for him, I felt to pray that Jesus would bind the devil "now." We continued to pray for his healing. He told us afterwards that as soon as the word "now" was spoken, the pain started to leave, and he recovered quite quickly. We had some distance to walk back to the house, and as we got close to the property, I suggested that we get the Elders to come and pray for him. We had only prayed for Jesus to bind the devil and as soon as I had spoken that out, he collapsed, unconscious. We prayed vehemently for his recovery, which seemed to take some time. We managed to get him back to the house where the leaders prayed for him. Later I asked God what had gone wrong, and I felt that He told me that He had given us authority, and that I had sown seeds of doubt by suggesting we needed the elders to pray. To this day as far as I know, that gentleman has kept good health.

I was quite involved with maintenance at the many Addict Houses and other properties around the area. One day I was sent to do a repair job that required cement, sand and some plumbing parts. The Chinese boys sent me to a local shop where the proprietors did not speak any English, and I did not speak any Cantonese. I eventually managed to buy all that I required by drawing pictures of what I needed, pantomiming mixing actions, and pointing to concrete outside the shop. I think the boys were quite surprised to see me back so soon! I was very thankful that my concreting job wasn't high up on one of the multi-storey buildings with rickety bamboo scaffolding to climb!

In January 1995 I was involved with levelling and replacing the piles that supported the Sanctuary building at Hang Fook Camp. The Sanctuary was a roof with no walls, where we had meals, gathered together, and held church services with up to 500 people attending. Sometimes with visiting evangelists, there could be up to 1,000 people with standing room only.

The support piles had been devoured by white ants (termites) and I was surprised that it still stood when I saw how much damage they had done. Many of the piles were completely eaten through, yet it had remained standing in spite of the storms. I started by replacing six of the piles by cutting off the destroyed parts, welding brackets to fit onto the concrete pads, and eventually replaced over fifty of them. It took a lot longer than it should have, as I was trying to involve the camp brothers. In many cases the brothers were far more qualified than I was, but after being addicts for so long, they did not have the confidence to take responsibility for the work. They were also involved in other programmes within Hang Fook Camp which did not leave much time for the pile replacement work.

We were also helped by visiting international naval crews from the UK and USA who donated their time and expertise in many ways. Like so many missions we were often frustrated by lack of materials to complete many of the jobs. We often took time to be with God and "pray in" the materials needed.

Pillar Point
When I had originally received the letter of invitation to Hong Kong from Jackie Pullinger, it had mentioned Pillar Point Refugee Camp, which was a detention centre containing Vietnamese refugees (largely comprised of "boat people"). This had touched my heart, and I had felt a special affinity for it. In

fact, I had felt God was calling me to work there. What I did not know was at that time the St Stephen's Society had not yet received permission and direction to oversee this refugee camp.

When Jackie had raced in on my first week to tell us about the United Nations giving us Pillar Point to manage, I had gone outside and wept at the greatness of God. Sometime later in the same year there was mention that some staff would be needed by the management team who were going to take over the operation of the Pillar Point refugee camp. I made myself known to the managers who asked me to go away and pray about joining the team. They also prayed about it and the consensus was that I should join them. I was then quite shocked when the St Stephen's Society decided that I was to stay with them at Hang Fook Camp, even though I was permitted to work part-time for St Stephen's management as a volunteer. I felt upset by this as I was certain that God had called me to work there. I retired to my room to ask God what it was all about. The first thing that He did was to lead me to the scripture about servants being obedient to their masters

> *Servants, be obedient to them that are your masters according to the flesh, with fear and trembling, in singleness of your heart, as unto Christ...* (Ephesians 6:5 KJV)

I felt God wanted me to be obedient to my masters without grumbling, so I prayed to Him and said that it was His problem and if He wanted me to work at Pillar Point, He would change the situation.

Approximately two months later, one of the leaders of the St Stephen's Society called me aside and asked whether I still wanted to work at Pillar Point, I replied, "Yes, that is where I believed God wanted me to be." And he said, "You are free to go as soon as the re-piling of the Sanctuary is finished." This took another month and I finished the work on the Sanctuary on my own, gratefully accepting help from the brothers as they were available.

The Pillar Point Camp had about 1,200 registered refugees when St Stephen's Society took over management. The buildings the residents lived in were mostly two and three story buildings with very basic facilities. They have been described as overcrowded, noisy, and dirty.

The camp was enclosed by high fences with barbed wire on top. Mind you, that didn't deter the very agile Vietnamese much. The fences were more for keeping undesirable people out, as our camp was described as an open camp, meaning that the residents were free to come and go as they wished. In the 1980s the camps were closed and the residents locked in, to discourage the numbers of illegal boat people seeking refuge in Hong Kong due to the unrest in South East Asia. But while I was there, quite a number of them lived and worked outside of the camp.

The management team at Pillar Point was led by a young Englishman, James Ginns (whose wife Belinda was Chinese), with Martin Sperring (also from the UK) as the assistant manager in charge of the office staff. The rest of the team was made up of the heads of departments: Dermot Stack (a Scotsman) – Head of Security; Peter Emmet (UK) – Maintenance; Fran Nguyen (UK) – overseeing community work with her husband, Truong (Vietnamese).

The Vietnamese refugees viewed the new management with suspicion for a start, especially when we started to insist that they obeyed the rules. Our company employed 18 former

British Army Nepalese Gurkhas to act as security guards and there were around 60 staff in total.

Each residential flat was 18 feet by eight feet with a kitchen/wash room four feet square, with whole families living and sleeping in the remaining area. These flats could house up to six adults and children, and where there were even larger families, they would be granted one and a half flats.

Many of the men, and some of the women, in the camp were drug addicts, had criminal records, or both. This was one of the main reasons that a lot of them were not eligible for residency in Hong Kong. When just one member of the family had engaged in criminal activities or drugs, this often prevented the family's innocent members from gaining residency, which I found very sad.

Vietnamese refugees living in the Pillar Point camp had different needs to the other addicts, as in almost every case their families were in danger while they were away – either for rehabilitation or employment. This made it very difficult when we were trying to get them off drugs, as they were constantly worrying about their families. They had good reason to be concerned, as the others in the refugee camp had little respect for the rights of women and families.

One of the pleasant things that I discovered moving across to Pillar Point was that I would be getting a wage for working full-time with the management team, but eventually I would have to move out of Hang Fook Camp as I would be working directly as a volunteer within the Society's areas.

In the meantime, I commuted back and forth to Hang Fook Camp each day enjoying a wonderful bus trip along the coast. I was able to observe progress on the huge new Tsing Ma 2.2 km suspension bridges across to Lantau Island, that would eventually link the new airport at Chek Lap Kok with Hong Kong, carrying both high-speed rail and road on the same bridge. It was amazing how quickly such a massive project proceeded. In the evenings on my return, I enjoyed seeing all the lights on the bridge and their reflection in the water.

Massively imposing by day and a twinkling span of lights by night, the Tsing Ma Bridge is an engineering marvel.[4]

My work at Pillar Point involved all sorts of maintenance work, including painting, electrical, grass cutting, mending doors and locks, renovating flats, unblocking drains, repairing the security fence, maintaining the fire hoses, water supply and many other tasks.

One day I got a piece of steel stuck in my eye, and I had to go to a specialist to have it removed. As I have very little vision in my other eye, it was quite a worrying time. When the steel was removed, a bandage was put over my eye, leaving me unable to see where I was going. Fortunately one of the brothers from Hang Fook Camp had come with me, and he led me home. Often I come across people who are very willing to help others, but seldom are able to receive help. I believe that until we are able to receive help from others, we are unable to receive the full benefit of help from Jesus.

One of the reasons that the St Stephen's Society was invited by the United Nations to be involved in Pillar Point was the drug problem. The St Stephen's Society had a reputation throughout the world for its successful work in rehabilitation of addicts. They asked God to do what man was unable to achieve and so we started an "Addicts meeting" in the camp to begin to sow God's seeds in these broken lives. Sadly, it was not as successful as the work with the Chinese, Europeans and other races. St Stephen's Society had made an interesting discovery in the English translation work that the Vietnamese had to be treated differently to the Chinese to achieve the same result. Despite some successes, we were unable to find the key to this problem.

When we started the addict meetings in the camp, we used one of the Vietnamese interpreters to speak to them, and for the first few meetings, he was always called to some disturbance or other just after the meeting had started. This of course disrupted the meetings. So one night I felt led to take two others out of the meeting to pray around the building, binding the work of the devil. From that time on, the interpreter was never again called away. One night I was asked to give the message to the meeting, and in my talk I was prompted to remind those there to look to the Lord for deliverance from drugs, rather than relying on the St Stephen's Society. Although I did not know at the time, two weeks later the meetings were stopped, and I again reminded the addicts to look to Jesus for deliverance from their drug addiction.

When I returned from my first holiday in New Zealand in September 1995, I moved out of Hang Fook Camp and moved into a flat near Tuen Mun Ferry Pier, sharing with Dermot Stack. Dermot had left behind a wife and family in Scotland, and at God's call had come to work in the camp looking after his beloved Gurkhas. He had been a Major in the British Army, and had spent much of his life in Hong Kong, working with the Gurkhas. He was able to speak Nepalese, among other languages. He often attended a Nepali Christian church and preached to them in their own language.

While inspecting a potential flat that suited us, I saw the lovely view from the main bedroom and thought it would be great to have it, but as Dermot had the senior position in the camp, I felt the main bedroom should be his. Dermot was very tall (6'4"), and greatly amused the Real Estate Agent by lying down on the floor to try the room for length, only to find that the room was too small for him. I was delighted to claim the main bedroom, while he barely managed to fit into the second bedroom. He had to sleep with his feet stretched out from the end of the bed, into the space created by the bay window. They don't build spaces for tall people! The flat cost us HK$5,000 per month (around NZ$100). At the time, the conversion was approximately twelve Hong Kong dollars to one New Zealand dollar.

I think God, with His usual sense of humour, put together a very tidy, retired British Army Major, and a very undisciplined and untidy Kiwi. I know it did me a lot of good and I suspect it was beneficial to Dermot as well. Fortunately we both had a sense of humour and we survived nearly a year of each other's company.

Dermot had not done a great deal of cooking, but he was determined to do his share, sometimes with unusual results. Often there would be frantic calls from the kitchen, "How do I measure four ounces of flour?" or some other similar question. One day he very bravely decided to cook us some lasagne. Some days previously he had put aside a box of flour with the right amount for his recipe. I had come to do some cooking and unable to find the flour, I had opened a new box and used a little out of it. Dermot came to make the sauce for the lasagne and grabbed the box that I had opened and poured it into his mix. A short time later there was a cry from the kitchen, "The sauce is too thick, what do I do?" "Add milk to thin it," I replied. A little while later, "I've run out of milk." "Use water," I called, then later again, "It's still too thick." I decided that I had better have a look, and after seeing this extremely thick and sticky mess we discovered what had happened. I used the excess flour mixture to make a cheese sauce for a cauliflower cheese recipe instead.

I saw the humour of the situation and started to laugh, and couldn't stop. Relations became rather strained, and fortunately there was a disturbance at the camp and Dermot had to rush off. When he returned I had managed to stop laughing, and he had remembered an occasion when he had been unable to stop laughing at a similar disaster that had happened to someone else. It was one of the things I admired about him, was his ability to laugh at himself.

On another occasion he was called to the camp, as one of the stall keepers had been involved in an incident involving drugs. The stall keeper's brother had been found to be carrying some straws of heroin at the camp. As he was arrested, he managed to throw them on the ground and all the Vietnamese children had dived to pick them up before the police did (without the evidence, the police would not have a case). The stall keeper had also got involved in the fracas and also got arrested. If he had been charged and convicted of a drug offence he would have been barred from re-settlement.

The wife of the stall keeper was very upset and threw a five-litre can of paint at Dermot – as Head of Security for the camp he got the blame for all that had happened. He was covered in paint from head to toe, and had to ride his bike through Tuen Mun back to the flat in that condition. It was the nearest that we came to a full-scale riot in all the time we were running the camp. Dermot was very gracious, forgiving the lady concerned and taking no further action.

Another time we came across one of the Vietnamese rushing around the camp, looking for a sledge hammer. When we asked why he wanted it, he said that while using the bathroom (a Chinese-style toilet with just a floor-level hole with automatic flushing), a large sum of money had accidentally fallen from his pocket as he crouched there, and had been flushed away. We felt it was poetic justice, as the money had most likely come from illegal drug dealing. He was feeling very flushed!

During the time Dermot and I shared a flat, we ran a weekly house group for the Christian staff members. In our meetings, we would pray for camp-related issues and for each other. One day during our prayers, we felt led to pray for the people running the camp stalls. Several days later, one of the stall proprietors rushed up to Fran, and asked to give his heart to the Lord. This man was a drug addict, and had been a very difficult person to deal with. His wife also became a Christian about a week later. Some time later, I was on a bus and saw this couple, but I did not recognise them with their huge smiles. I had never seen them smiling before, and it wasn't until they had got off the bus, that I worked out who they were.

Sadly for us, Dermot eventually left to go and rejoin his family. He had offered his services to help just to set up the camp security, and stayed on for 18 months. We all missed him and his humour.

The St Stephen's Society had a two-year contract to manage the camp, which we felt was the duration God intended for our involvement. When the contract ended in 1996, we withdrew, finding it difficult given the significant improvements we had made since taking over the camp. The decision sparked doubts about whether we had correctly perceived God's will. One Tuesday, a senior member of the staff came and asked that exact question. As we prayed about it, I suggested to him that if he secured a new job by week's end and was overjoyed about it, that would confirm God's desire for us to withdraw. By Friday, the staff member came to me, excited to report that he had indeed found a new position.

Leaving was difficult, but we took comfort in God's promise to be there for the refugees when they sought Him. We had planted the seeds of Christianity in the camp, leaving the harvest to God.

While I was working in the camp, the Gurkhas would constantly ask me why, at my age, I was working hard and not sitting at home letting my children look after me. At that time I was only 56 years old. I kept sharing with them that God had called me to the work and that was why I was there. Eventually they started to ask me about God, and this gave us an opportunity to give them Nepalese Bibles. Then in their broken English they would ask me lots of questions relating to the Bible. When I couldn't answer their questions, I encouraged them to seek God's guidance, and I am sure that God gave them answers as they returned with more questions! They lived in a communal setting, sharing Bibles amongst themselves.

They lived in Tuen Mun, about three miles away. They ran to work, worked a 12-hour shift, and at the end of each shift ran as a group all the way home. I was very grateful for their companionship and presence.

Tuen Mun

After the church at Hang Fook Camp was closed, three Vineyard churches were started and it became difficult for me to get to their services every week as it involved up to four hours travelling to and from the three-hour services. So, I decided on the weeks that I had to work six days, that I would attend a local Anglican church that had just started in the area.

After going along for several services, I noticed that the minister was very flustered just before each service, and I felt that God wanted me to get alongside him and offer encouragement. So I went up and asked if he had anyone pray for him before the service. He suddenly threw his hands in the air in realisation, and exclaimed, "I'm mad, I'm mad!" and immediately asked me to pray for him, and the service. I had been doing this for several weeks, when I felt that God was asking me to draw back from praying with him, so when I did not turn up early enough to pray, he got his Elders to pray with him. Another thing that God showed was to pray where He wanted me to sit during the service. Every time I did that, there was always a person that God wanted me to minister to. This has also occurred in other churches.

Hard Lessons

One day I was sitting in church at Hang Fook Camp beside a young couple, who I knew well, when I felt God saying to me, "Spirit of Fear," about the wife. I asked the husband a few questions as to whether there was any reason for fear in their family. It turned out that his wife had just found out that she was pregnant again, and because she had a miscarriage in the past, she was fearful of having another one. I prayed with them that day, and became very closely involved with them. They also sought counselling from others and as the pregnancy progressed they discovered more setbacks. The unborn baby was a boy, and tests showed that he had Edwards Disease, a very severe form of Spina Bifida, so they dedicated the baby in the womb to God. The doctor that they were seeing recommended that she have the pregnancy terminated. This was firmly rejected. They did a lot of research on the disease and found other babies who had been born, and found out how to care for them. They visited a home for these children and became very involved with them. Many people around the world became involved in prayer for this little boy and everyone expected a miracle.

I spent quite a lot of time with the couple, often going to stay with them. I was staying with them at the time the baby was due, and it stopped moving in the womb. They were extremely concerned and went off to see the specialist, and sadly it was confirmed that the baby had died. Naturally they were very upset.

They had a memorial service for the baby a little while later, and again I was asked to stay with them. After everyone had gone home and we were trying to console each other, I felt that God was telling me that they would welcome a child into their family within a year, but I felt that it would not be their biological one. I sensed that God was prompting me to tell this couple they would have a child of their own in the future. After seeking confirmation from God multiple times, I eventually shared this message with them. However, they struggled to believe it, as they were deeply angry with God for allowing their son to die.

Later that year they went for a holiday in another country, and God started to bring healing in their hearts. They returned to Hong Kong and miraculously they were able to adopt a baby boy within the year. At that time in Hong Kong there was a three-year waiting list for adoptions! A while later the wife became pregnant again, and we were delighted when the mother successfully delivered her own healthy child. I have kept in touch with them over the years and their family continues to grow, having several of their own children.

Hong Kong

Christmas

One day a group of us had gone to visit Pillar Point to pray around it. We were praying with an addict who had spent some time in one of the New Boy Houses, when a lady burst into the room and asked if she could give her heart to Jesus. It was quite complicated as she only spoke Vietnamese, I only spoke English, and my Chinese friend spoke English and Cantonese, so we had to use the Vietnamese addict as an interpreter to translate from Vietnamese to Cantonese, with my friend then translating to English. Eventually we were able to lead her through confession, and acceptance of Jesus. Later we managed to get a Vietnamese pastor to visit her, and he asked her a lot of questions. She was married to another Vietnamese drug addict, and she had a young baby. One of the questions was how they supported themselves. She burst into tears and said, "My husband steals." Her husband also used to beat her to get the money that she earned when she started back at work. A year or so later, she had taken enough, and finally left him. She later went to live with a Chinese man outside of the camp. We had great difficulty in knowing how to pray for her, but were sympathetic because of her circumstances. We did continue to pray for her, even though we lost touch.

Much later, at the end of my stay in Hong Kong, I was going to a Tuen Mun church service on the last Sunday before Christmas. As I alighted from the train, this same lady was getting off at the same stop, and meeting with one of the camp social workers. She had left the Chinese man and returned to her husband, who had not reformed at all. It transpired that she was coming to the church service, and the social worker was arranging for her to go into a women's refuge outside of the camp. I felt that God had brought her back, because of her commitment. So I felt that God had shown me that he was looking after her, which was like a Christmas present to me.

Wedding

While I was in Hong Kong, and working in one of the New Boy Houses, I had felt to say to the young lady that was in charge that I would come to her wedding. She had welcomed the idea, although at that stage she had no immediate plans to be married. Four years later I was on my way back to England through Hong Kong, and staying with a close friend when I found out that she was getting married the upcoming weekend in England. My friends urged me to go, using their invitation, which they were unable to use. So I decided to attend. In the middle of the service she turned around and saw me there, and she burst into tears. She was delighted that I had come, and even had the best man welcome me as a special guest.

Meals

One of the things that gave me a lot of pleasure was to take people out for a meal when I could afford to. One evening I was taking a young lady from Hang Fook Camp out to dinner. We were walking along a street, when with a squeal, she suddenly jumped into my arms. I did catch her, but I was very surprised. It turned out that some repairs were being made to the street, and they had disturbed a family of young rats, and one had run up her leg! On many of the occasions that I was prompted to take someone out to dinner, it often turned out that there were issues that needed to be dealt with.

The St Stephen's Society agreement was to run the camp for two years, as that came to an end, I felt that it was time to leave. The camp was being handed over to a non-Christian organisation, and in addition, the British were handing Hong Kong and its Territories back to the Chinese government, and there was a lot of uncertainty.

My two and a half years in Hong Kong was an incredible time of personal growth and I learnt that I can do so many things that I thought I couldn't. I learned to trust and rely on God for my own needs, as well as the needs of others. When stuck, I found if you ask God, He will give you a picture of how to go about it. I learnt how to relate to people better, especially with language barriers, even though I thought I was just a quiet farmer.

It was a first-hand, sometimes confronting, experience of seeing how displaced people were living, and in their disadvantaged state, had been exploited. I observed first-hand, the scourge of drug addiction, but also the hand of God in their recovery. I saw the poorest living conditions of refugees against a background of some marvellous engineering projects.

All of these experiences opened my eyes and gave me a lot of wisdom to deal with the next stage of my life. And in fulfilment of an earlier prophecy, many of the Vietnamese I worked with saw me as a father figure, which I rather enjoyed.

It was both with sadness and relief that I made arrangements to leave Hong Kong when my visa was about to expire.

SIX
NEW ZEALAND FURLOUGH

Have I not commanded you? Be strong and of good courage; do not be afraid, nor be dismayed, for the Lord your God is with you wherever you go. (Joshua 1:9)

On January 9, 1997, I departed Hong Kong. B Jai, a former maintenance manager at Pillar Point, picked me up from James's house and drove me to the airport. B Jai now owned a taxi business. Unfortunately I encountered a series of setbacks. Firstly, the airline had overbooked the flight and my seat was cancelled, despite asking my travel agent to confirm the booking. Fortunately, I was found a seat on an Air New Zealand flight that was due to leave immediately. Next, I was stopped by Immigration as my visa had expired on December 31st.

When trying to renew it, I found out that the immigration office had moved locations, and I was unable to get to the new office before it closed. Anyway, the immigration people detained me in a room for 45 minutes, asking the same questions over and over. I was very calm and spent much of the time praying. Finally they let me go, but not before they charged me $115 for a visa to cover the nine days that I had overstayed. The plane took off immediately after I boarded and I believe that they delayed the plane for me.

The day after I arrived back in New Zealand, James and his wife Belinda (the former managers from Pillar Point) also arrived from Hong Kong, and we all stayed with my friends Mary and Derek Graham. I had just (that day) purchased a small car from a friend. James and Belinda wanted to tour Northland, and as he had not brought his British driving licence (only his Hong Kong one), he was unable to rent a car. So I lent him my very ordinary car and I was loaned a delightful sports car to drive until mine was returned.

Making plans for my furlough, I arranged to rent a small flat in Papakura rather than disturb any of my tenants. I bought myself a mobile phone with data and fax capabilities so I could keep in touch with family and friends. It wasn't worth installing a permanent phone line for what I believed would be a short period.

Returning from over two years in Hong Kong, I felt quite burnt out, though I didn't realise it at the time. I believed God wanted me to take at least a three-month holiday, as the longest break I'd ever had was just two weeks, apart from an occasional overseas trip. I wondered how I would fill all that free time.

I tried playing a game of golf with a friend, but as I swung the club I pulled a muscle in my back. As we prayed for healing, we felt God say that if I didn't rest, He would make sure that I did. My friend felt that he was getting a message from God too, and he shared the same words with me. Much to my surprise, I needed every bit of the time to rest.

At Mercy Missions' request, I spent a few days driving and delivering food for them, when they were short-staffed. Once the initial fatigue subsided, I was able to reach out and spend time with some people in need. Other friends were incredibly kind, and I received numerous dinner invitations. During this period, I reconnected with most of my friends and family.

I had a good rest and started to write *The Recycled Teen*.

During my time at home, I met a young couple who had believed they had been called to a specific mission. After a lot of prayer, and approval from their church, they were all packed and ready to go, when the mission organisation informed them they were no longer needed.

This unexpected rejection dealt a blow to their confidence, which was further undermined by some church members suggesting they may not have truly heard God's calling. Discouraged, they retreated inward and were unsure of their next steps. Sensing their struggle, I gently suggested that perhaps the mission organisation had made a mistake, and that the Devil might be trying to derail their plans. I encouraged them to seek the Lord's guidance on the path He had for them. After much prayer, they started a new ministry within their own community that was highly successful. Later, the husband trained to be a pastor and now leads a church of his own.

A friend's wife had recently left him so I visited him at his work to offer support. He was devastated, and I identified with his pain. I offered to have dinner with him, where he poured out his heart and vented his frustrations. After listening for a while, I started sharing stories and asking questions to help shift his bitterness. I suggested while we can't change others, we can change ourselves. He came to realise that he had a very special wife whom he loved dearly, and now felt hurt and betrayed by her departure. We spent time in prayer, asking God to reveal areas for his own growth and change. Afterwards I managed to find a Christian woman to encourage his wife. Eventually they decided to give their marriage another try, and I am pleased to say that many years later, they were still happily together.

After a couple of months at home, I was ready to start planning my next adventure. Two years prior, when my time with Mercy Missions had come to a close, I received invitations to work with both St Stephen's Society in Hong Kong, and also Youth With a Mission (YWAM). I now felt called to serve with YWAM. My good friend Mary Graham gave me a contact for YWAM in Harpenden, England, so after some thought and prayer, I contacted them.

Next, I applied to the British High Commission for an ancestry certificate (as my grandparents had been born in the UK) so that I could get a visa to work in Great Britain for YWAM. I was not sure where God would lead me from there but I wanted to be free to come and go. I booked a ticket to London on the information given to me by some of the staff at the visa office, who indicated it should be no problem. The travel agent kept checking that it was progressing as informed. A week before I was due to fly out, I had a phone call that my application had been turned down. The person who called to inform me gave me no explanation as to why it had been declined. I asked that he keep my papers as I would try to find some more information.

I had to delay my flight. I prayed about it, and after two weeks felt God tell me to go to Wellington. So I caught the overnight train, and was at the British High Commission office waiting on the step until the office opened. I had gathered a lot more information to present. I went in and told them that I had come about my visa. The lady went off to get the papers and I heard the official sounds of approval – stamping on papers. She came out and handed me the passport, and told me that I already had my visa. She did not ask to see any further documentation. I must admit with all the difficulty that I had I wondered if God was shutting the door, but often obstacles are put in front of us which we have to overcome to show our dedication and commitment to the path.

As I was due to leave New Zealand, Joanne, my youngest daughter, was having trouble with headaches and her left eye was bloodshot and bulging. The doctors diagnosed an aneurysm behind the eye. As my plane departed, I was crying because she was so sick and I was apprehensive that I would not see her again. God had told me to go, and I had argued with Him. Eventually I felt God promise He would look after her. My faith was at a very low ebb and I spent a lot of time praying for her. I'm happy to report her eye was successfully repaired with some extremely delicate surgery.

SEVEN
ENGLAND

And a servant of the Lord must not quarrel but be gentle to all, able to teach, patient, in humility correcting those who are in opposition, if God perhaps will grant them repentance, so that they may know the truth... (2 Timothy 2: 24-25)

I arrived in England at the end of August 1997, and started work for Youth with a Mission (YWAM) at Harpenden straight away. Harpenden is a town 30 minutes by train northwest of London in the county of Hertfordshire.

The YWAM base had 48 acres, of which about a third was covered by the Oval and surrounding buildings, known as Harpenden Oval. It had been a National Children's home (for orphan children), that had run a commercial printing business among other things to help fund it. The rest of the property consisted of a large grass area which contained a soccer pitch, and an area of mature woods. The buildings were mostly brick with tiled roofs and had two stories totalling 109,000 square feet of floor space. A main rail line ran across the bottom of the property and along one side. There was a small cemetery in the bottom corner, in which there were many young children buried from the various epidemics. The Oval was a beautifully grassed area, with a road going right around it. Beyond the road it is surrounded by mature trees, with all of the buildings forming the outer oval.

Sometimes you could see deer grazing on the rough ground and if you were very lucky, you might see a fox sneaking past. In springtime, there would be a carpet of bluebells transforming the woodland floor into a delicate sea of blue. There were quite a number of birds, including a few pheasants. Pigeons roosted in the eaves of the buildings and were quite a pest. Between the railway and our entrance, a model railway club had several hundred metres of track and I used to enjoy going to see their open days.

There was a lovely stone chapel at the head of the Oval, which is used by YWAM for six days of the week, and by the local Bethany Church on Sundays. Some of the buildings were quite run down but others had been renovated over the years. The old Factory building was completely derelict when I went there and was only used for storage. There was a large dining room with a well-equipped kitchen, which I discovered was generally under-used. Later a small coffee area was added in one corner of the dining room for the residents and workers.

There were about 150 permanent staff who lived on the base, and the numbers could go up to about 220 when there were discipleship schools running. There were quite a number of staff who lived off the base, and there were local day workers who came in to help.

I was accommodated in building number 7. Within the building there were five families (17 family members), eight single girls, and six single men. The families were strategically placed to keep us all in order. We had three other similar buildings, two were used for staff and one was used to house the

Discipleship school students. I was sharing a room with a helpful and industrious young man.

When I arrived, I joined the maintenance team, who were hard at work renovating half of building number four, so that some families could move in. It had been partly destroyed by fire which meant that a lot of work needed doing. The ceilings needed repairing, walls re-plastering and painting, and the floors had to be taken up and re-laid. With all this work the fixtures had to be renewed, skirtings and architraves replaced. All the plumbing and electrical wiring had to be replaced, and all of this was the job of the maintenance team. I was set to work helping them with it all. God with his usual sense of humour had me doing finishing work, including painting and beautifying one of the refurbished buildings. I had always managed to avoid that type of work in the past as I disliked it, and would prefer more practical building work.

My new boss, Ken Hudson, was a retired engineer with a large range of skills. It was seldom that I saw him baffled by any problem on the base. He and his wife Mary, had been involved with YWAM for a number of years. Ken had a passionate love of Citroën cars, which he seemed to collect, having three of them at one time. Mary had started the very successful YWAM bookshop on the base and it was later taken over by John Clark. Ken was a great teacher and enabled me to learn many new skills. He loved outreach and enjoyed the challenges of working with staff from many nations.

I enjoyed my physical work immensely, learning many new skills from Ken, but spiritually I felt I was in a very dry place for a long time. Later, I discovered by reading my diaries that God had really blessed the time and had spent days talking to me during my quiet times. There had been a couple of unfortunate incidents at the base, and they were being very cautious in who they allowed to pray for others. I felt that this was hindering them spiritually. Though I found it difficult to start with, I wanted to be obedient to my masters.

> *Have confidence in your leaders and submit to their authority, because they keep watch over you as those who must give an account.* (Hebrews 13:17a NIV)

At Christmas time I was asked to house-sit for some new friends. While I was staying in their place, I was far enough removed from the base to be able to pray clearly about the matter. I cried out to God in my frustration, asking Him to remedy the situation, and to help me to find favour with the YWAM leadership.

A few days later I invited one of the leaders to a meal at a restaurant, and afterwards he asked if he could discuss a personal matter with me. We went back to the house I was staying in, had a long discussion and ended up praying together. Another leader then affirmed my walk with God. Then about a week later, to my amazement, I was asked by the YWAM leadership to come on staff on a longer-term basis. This was a surprise, as normally you would only be accepted to work for a period of three months, unless you had completed YWAM's Discipleship Training School lecture and outreach phases – which I had not done.

About that time one of the ministries in Harpenden had closed down, due to lack of finance. One of my friends had worked with them and now had no other ministry to go to. After a while the leadership asked him to leave. He was very hurt and upset and I spent a considerable time ministering to him. He was upset about the closure of the ministry as well as being asked to leave. Eventually I felt to say to him that I did not feel the actions were against him personally but rather that they needed the space for others who belonged to operating teams. I suggested that he go and see the personnel officer to clarify the situation. He found that he was not rejected and that they were able to recommend him to another base that ran a ministry that was close to his heart.

One of the tasks that needed doing on the base was to rake up all the autumn leaves. A lot can be learnt about others when you are raking up a large area of leaves. Some people pass by and offer encouragement, commenting on what a good job that you are doing, or how nice it looks where you have finished. Others are discouragers, saying things like, "What a terrible job, you must get bored," or "You have a long way to go." Then there are those who completely ignore the gardener, often looking away as they walk by, perhaps out of a guilty conscience. This applies to just about any task that you undertake.

Another of my tasks was to supervise the DTS (Disciple Training School) students as they spent two hours a day helping with practical work. On the whole they seemed to enjoy the experience, even though often the work was hard physical labour. The girls were expected to help as well, and if at all possible, I would work alongside them. This often became a time of sharing, and sometimes, ministry with them, as we worked together.

Working in the maintenance department, I was not directly involved in the spiritual training of the students. However, being able to witness their growth was incredibly fulfilling. God allowed me to see them mature in their walk with Him, which

I found very rewarding. By sharing personal experiences and stories from my time in Hong Kong, I could provide practical examples of my own spiritual growth and trust in God.

A place I received spiritual fulfilment was with the Bethany Church that I attended on most Sundays. Sometimes God would give me a word for an individual, and sometimes for the church. One particular day, I felt that I had a word for the church, but I did not speak it out, and felt that I had missed what God had wanted me to do. At the end of the service the minister pointed to me and asked me to close the meeting, and I was able to speak it out. To my knowledge the minister had never done that before.

Soon after joining the church, I felt that a couple had become victims of a family curse. I shared my concerns with the minister, who agreed. The minister then called the couple over and we prayed with them. This turned out to be correct, as the wife's Muslim parents disapproved of their daughter becoming a Christian. Despite this, the couple had a strong ministry in the church.

Another time, a woman in the congregation came to me in tears, explaining that her husband had forbidden her from attending church. While I felt inclined to advise her to be obedient to her husband, I recognised that God would know her heart, as her husband was not a Christian at the time. Instead, I suggested she pray and ask God to help her behave in a Christ-like manner toward her husband. Several weeks later, she returned to church accompanied by her husband. A few more weeks passed before he committed his life to the Lord and became an active member of the congregation.

During a lunch at the YWAM base, John Clark, a long-serving YWAM team member, invited me to sit with him and a young man. This young man expressed a desire for God's power, yet was unwilling to give his heart to the Lord. To my surprise, he openly revealed that he was a practising Satanist, and dressed in dark clothing and a long black coat. John spent a lot of time talking with him and encouraging him to change his ways. I spent most of the time praying, observing that it is impossible to serve two masters.

There was quite an amount of concern about him on the base. One group suggested that he should not be allowed there, but we pointed out to them that Christ's power is stronger than the Devil's. In a Mission Builders prayer meeting we prayed for wisdom in dealing with this young man. After leaving the base I later learned, with the guidance of many people, this man was eventually led to the Lord, confessing his sins and renouncing the power that the Devil had over his life.

In our maintenance department, at times, a particular leader felt that he had the right to help himself to supplies for his own personal use. Ken, the manager, changed the locks on the workshop, and then instructed me not to provide that leader with keys. Ken wanted to monitor usage, and prevent removal of supplies that he had bought in especially for a particular project.

One day, the fellow became frustrated to find the workshop locked after Ken had changed the locks. He came to me for the keys, which I reluctantly provided as I was occupied with another task at the time. The fellow returned the keys late in the day, raising my suspicion that he had made a copy. I immediately informed Ken, and we prayed that God would reveal the truth. About a week later, the fellow admitted to having a workshop key, which Ken confirmed he had not provided.

Initially, I considered confronting him, but then decided to wait. A day or two later, the apologetic leader approached us and confessed. Previously, I had advised him to be diligent in the small matters, recommending that he purchase his own supplies. He had responded (with a hint of accusation) that my standards were almost religious, but later acknowledged the need to change his ways.

While I was in Harpenden, I received a letter from Mercy Missions in New Zealand, informing me that my dear friend Rex had been diagnosed with inoperable stomach cancer. The letter asked me and many others to pray for him. I had started my mission journey with Rex and his wife Barb, who had founded Mercy Missions in the early 1990s.

About three months later, one evening I felt strongly compelled to call Rex. Though I initially procrastinated, I soon sensed God telling me to "Ring Rex now!" When I called, it turned out to be the only time that day I could have reached him – he had been haemorrhaging during the night and was waiting for an ambulance to take him to the hospital. Thankfully, he recovered from that scare.

Fortunately I was able to see Rex one last time when I returned to New Zealand much later, although by then he was very unwell, had lost a lot of weight and only appeared to be skin and bone. When I first arrived back, he asked me whether I would be a Pall Bearer at his funeral. I said yes, but qualified it as I was only home for a month, and due to fly back to England. I managed to see a lot of Rex during that time, and was even able to be with him the night before he died.

Rex was always a great encourager, and he spent all of the last years of his life trying to introduce others to the Jesus that he loved. In the final week before he passed, I was privileged to watch him teaching a class of new disciples from the video "Viva Christo Rea" and encouraging his students to get to know

England

the Christ that he loved and served. In that same week he also allowed TV3 to interview him about the achievements of Mercy Missions in South Auckland, which was later broadcast on television.

By delaying my flight back to the UK for four days, I was able to carry out my duties at the funeral, which was a celebration of his going home to the Lord. I was very thankful to Qantas and their staff who were so accommodating and helpful in rearranging my flights.

On the same trip, I was hoping to stay with some good friends in Hong Kong, but had been unable to get hold of them. When I landed in Hong Kong, I still did not know whether I had a place to stay or not. I had been trying to get in touch with them from New Zealand without success. I rang them from the airport, and they had just walked in the door after arriving back from overseas themselves and so I had a bed for the night. This was yet another occasion where God had His hand in the arrangements.

While I was home in New Zealand for that month, I got an email to say that Ken Hudson (from the YWAM base) had a heart attack. After thinking and praying for a long time I felt I needed to commit to my time in New Zealand. When I got back to the YWAM base, I was asked to take over the responsibilities of Maintenance Manager. I did so on the condition that when Ken recovered that I would relinquish the position to him. I found out later that Ken's heart attack occurred while he was visiting someone in hospital, and he was immediately given treatment. It seems divine intervention saved him, for had this occurred elsewhere, he likely would not have survived.

After I had returned to England, and not long after Ken's heart attack, it was his and Mary's 60th birthdays, but due to

Ken's health they had not had any celebrations. So I thought that I would arrange a party to honour them, but knowing Ken, I knew it would be very hard to do this without him becoming suspicious, so instead I invited them to a quiet dinner to celebrate.

They arrived at my place and were a little surprised that the table wasn't set, and all that I appeared to be cooking was a large pot of rice, but still they did not suspect anything. They assumed that we would eat in a small coffee bar attached to the main hall on the base.

For the surprise, I had invited 60 people, and also organised the local Chinese takeaway restaurant to supply us with food. I had also asked the people who had been invited to have either a testimony about his work, or some funny stories to tell about him. When Ken and I arrived at the main hall we opened the door, and they were quite overcome by the surprise reception. As for the stories about Ken, they were a bit slow getting started, so I told amusing incidents about the other guests, and shared stories about Ken and Mary until they got the message. The evening was a lot of fun and a great success.

One night, I was invited to speak to a cell group from the church. I asked God what He wanted shared, and I felt that He wanted me to speak on prophesy. As I had not spoken on this before, I was quite apprehensive and I asked for confirmation. During the day as I worked with some of the students on work duties, one of them shared with me some scriptures that confirmed my topic for that night's meeting. After I had finished my lesson, I suggested they practice what they had been taught about encouraging others through prophecy. They took turns prophesying to each other. The man who spoke with me unexpectedly repeated the same prophetic words that I had received in New Zealand six years prior. This seemed impossible, as there was no way he could have known those words. The other prophecies were also inspired, revealing they originated from God, not human sources.

While I was working in England, I received an email from my brother Ron, in New Zealand. He explained that his youngest son had asked him to go to a church function that his son was involved with. While my brother was there, he was welcomed by the church members, and found it enjoyable and decided to return for another service. He was invited to join an Alpha course – an outline of core Christian principles – and at its conclusion he felt to give his heart to the Lord. This of course delighted me, and his son. I and many others had been praying for him for some time. Ron was baptised on 6th December 1998.

One long weekend, I decided to go and visit Brighton in the south of England, as I had never been there before. It rained most of the time that I was there, but I had a really good rest which is what I had needed. It was good to see the famous Brighton pier, although I was not too impressed with all the "One Armed Bandit" gambling machines. I was quite taken with the display of the small boats that they had used for the rescue of the troops from Dunkirk. Whilst still in Brighton I went out for dinner, and I was looking for a Chinese meal under six pounds, so I asked God which way to go. He directed me up a street that did not appear to have any open shops on it, and very few lights. At the next street I felt that I was directed to turn right, but the only shop light was on my left. I investigated it and found that it was an Indian Restaurant. I was finally obedient and turned right, and after walking some distance, I found the Chinese Restaurant with the meal slightly under the price I had asked for!

The Recycled Teen

A task that I did on a regular basis was to collect the food donated by Marks and Spencer, a large department store chain. This reminded me of my work in South Auckland with Mercy Missions. This task involved taking a van to nearby St Albans, loading the food and delivering it back to the base, where it was shared out among all those who lived on the base. It was an enjoyable time for me as I was able to spend time praying as I drove.

Back at the base, we were always short of helpers for the maintenance department, yet we always seemed to manage to get all the necessary jobs done. Many people helped our team and some would come great distances just to help for a few weeks. We had electricians, plasterers, carpenters, refrigeration engineers, mechanical engineers, painters and many others. We were all involved in many of the jobs, and on occasion I helped out with the electrical tasks. In Hong Kong I had also faced a few electrical problems, and their electricity systems were based on the British system so we had worked them out. In England I observed the power points looked similar, however when working on them I realised with a shock that both ends of the system were live!

Years before, in New Zealand, I had asked a very successful mechanic how he was able to diagnose problems with cars that other mechanics had been unable to find. He told me that he always asked God, and often his eyes would be drawn to the part with the problem. This way he was able to fix it. While I was working at Harpenden I was frequently asked to deal with things that I had never had any experience with before. Usually after trying in my own strength and getting nowhere, I would finally ask God, and He would show me what to do.

On the base there were many different types of boiler systems, including coal, oil, and computer-controlled electric ones. We were mostly able to fix these ourselves, however one malfunctioned, and despite many attempts and much prayer, we could not fix it. Eventually we had to call in professional repairers, who took six weeks to resolve the problem.

Swiss Church Team
In 1998 we had a team from a church in Schaffhausen, Switzerland, come to help us with maintenance on the base. The Swiss church team were excellent workers and willing to do any jobs that we gave them, including helping with the renovation and painting of buildings. They had also cut hedges, pruned trees, picked up stones and built parking bays. I was working with a group of their girls picking up stones so that the gang mowers would not be damaged and as I worked, I felt compelled to share an inspiring message that I had heard many years ago. I spoke about how we are all created beautifully and uniquely created in God's sight. As I shared these words, I noticed one girl in particular seemed deeply affected due to her low self-esteem. Later, I learned she had shared the message with leaders to verify its authenticity. After she did this, I was asked to share my testimony with the entire group because of sharing that message.

In January 1999 I was invited to go to Switzerland to visit the team from the church who had helped us at Harpenden. I had a wonderful time with them and they took me to see many of their sights. I felt thoroughly spoilt. I had the joy of flying the length of Switzerland, seeing the snow-capped mountains either side of the plane before landing in Zurich. I was picked up at the airport and driven to Schaffhausen, passing through a small part of Germany along the way. The outreach group from that particular church was unique, as they had stayed together for over a year, and were the only group from the church to have undertaken such a mission.

That February, Jan von Rosenstiel, whom I had met while we worked together for St Stephen's Society in Hong Kong, visited me. During his stay, Jan discussed the gift of tongues with one of my flatmates, leaving quite an impression. Just four days after Jan's departure, that flatmate received the gift of tongues, a remarkable change from his previous skepticism and doubt about its value. He now ministers in Brazil.

Call to Mercy Ships

In July 1998, while serving at YWAM in Harpenden, I sensed God prompting me to resign by February 1999. Wanting a clear confirmation about this six-month timeline, I shared my impression with Ken, my supervisor. Though initially upset, Ken later apologised and gave me his blessing to leave. A few days later, Ken excitedly told me that an American had expressed interest in joining the base around the time I was set to depart. I took this as the confirmation I had sought from God about the timing of my departure.

At that time I asked God if I could have a month's holiday before I left there. Once news had spread, several people approached me and asked what I was going to do, and as I did not have an answer, they were telling me that I should just make things happen! I explained that since God had directed me to complete my work in Harpenden, I trusted He would reveal the next step. If He did not provide a plan, I would return to New Zealand and wait there for His guidance.

The beginning of February 1999 arrived, and I still had no idea of what God wanted of me.

EIGHT
AFRICA MERCY

February 1999 arrived, and my path forward was still a mystery. One evening I was invited to a pancake party. One of the people at the party was Donovan Palmer, who asked me what I was going to be doing after leaving the base. I replied that I did not know, but I had an invitation to go to a church in Bulgaria, but didn't have any details of what would be expected of me there. I had also been offered the opportunity to lead an "impact" team to Uganda. Donovan then asked me if I would be interested in helping with a new ship for Mercy Ships. Though I immediately had many questions, Donovan suggested we discuss it further in private, at a later time.

Mercy Ships is an international Christian ministry founded by YWAM in 1978:

> *Loren Cunningham had a long-time vision of a ship ministry, which was finally realised in 1979. The first ship, named* Anastasis *(the Greek word for Resurrection), became the first in a fleet to be known as Mercy Ships – a ministry which would provide hope and healthcare to the needy in port cities around the world.*[5]

They operate the largest non-governmental hospital ships in

> the world, that are staffed by volunteer doctors, nurses and other support staff. At this time, they had the Anastasis in operation, but had plans for a new ship to operate off the coast of Africa, improving the quality of life for people living with the diseases of poverty, disfigurement, and disability. The Anastasis served as the flagship of the Mercy Ships fleet from 1979–2007. It was the first civilian-owned hospital ship, serving marginalised communities, and those trapped in poverty. Ships are preferred so they can provide the clean and sterile environment necessary for surgical intervention, and they can be easily moved to different ports as required.[6]

When I finally caught up with Donovan, I discovered that they did not yet have a new ship, but were looking for one. Interestingly, the inter-island ferry *Maori* that I had travelled on back in my late teens between the North and South Islands of New Zealand, was one of the ships that YWAM had considered as a potential hospital ship many years earlier.

Even though a new ship was not yet available, I felt that time was right to pursue joining the Mercy Ships team. I filled in an application, and then some weeks later in early March, Jim Paterson and Brian Sloane interviewed me for a position. They asked me about joining the *Anastasis* specifically for an air conditioning project, telling me that they had not yet obtained the new ship. I agreed to take on whatever role they wanted me to do, but voiced my preference for the new ship. After the interview, I went back to my room, and I had a restless night, and concluded God did not want me to join the *Anastasis* at that time. The next morning, I returned to Mercy Ships and told them I did not feel called to the *Anastasis*, but would honour my commitment if they held me to it.

Africa Mercy

I spent considerable time praying about Mercy Ships, and as I was praying, I felt that Donovan was supposed to lead the project. Earlier he had told me that someone else was supposed to lead it. When I told him what I had felt, he looked a bit taken aback, and told me that the person who had been going to lead it, had turned it down. God had already been challenging him to take that position.

On March 25, 1999, I heard that a new ship had been acquired, but I heard no further details other than it would be docked at Newcastle upon Tyne in the north of England. Later I found I needed to fill in another form for Mercy Ships that I had overlooked. Almost two weeks later, on April 1st, Tamara Goodwin – Donovan's personal assistant – rang me to ask if I could be available to take a phone call from Donovan at 1520 hours. He called while at sea on the new ship, and asked me to join them on Sunday April 4th at Newcastle upon Tyne and, by the way, would I be able to drive a bus up, bringing the official photographer with me?

The date that I was due at Newcastle upon Tyne was also the same day I wanted to be "sent out" by Bethany Church, which I had been attending while I was in Harpenden. However, the time that Mercy Ships needed me in Newcastle meant that I would have had to leave Harpenden before this special service started. Fortunately the photographer that I was taking to Newcastle had been working late the night before, so he didn't want to leave until just after midday, so happily, I was able to attend the service.

At the church service there were a number of people from a DTS (Discipleship Training School) in Montana, USA. They had been supposed to go to Kosovo in the Balkans on outreach, but because of the war there, they had been refused entry, and they were all at a loose end wondering what to do next. Some of them gathered around, as I was prayed for, and also became interested in Mercy Ships.

I collected the photographer, and the drive was quite eventful as I had never been to that part of England before. While the photographer knew the main roads, he had little idea of where we were to go in Newcastle. Eventually we found our way to the ship at the Cammell Laird yard in Hebburn on the River Tyne.

The ship was called the *Dronning Ingrid* (Queen Ingrid, in Danish) and she was a former rail ferry built in Denmark in 1980 for the Danish State Railways (DSB). It was purchased for USD $6.5 million for Mercy Ships with funds donated from the Balcraig Foundation, run by a Scottish woman, Dame Ann Gloag.

> *Ann Gloag is a volunteer on a one-of-a-kind floating hospital Mercy Ship on which she is a volunteer with a mop and a broom. There are other volunteers with similar chores. So what is so unusual about Ms Gloag doing these necessary menial chores? She is the richest woman in Scotland, one of the wealthiest in the UK and founder of the multimillion pound Stagecoach Empire. Ms Gloag, a former nurse, has become a guardian angel of Mercy, donating 4 million pounds, the biggest donation Mercy Ships has received in its history, to help build a Mercy Ship. The* Africa Mercy *is the first addition in a proposed new plan to add ships to the existing fleet of floating hospitals that visit more than 70 ports worldwide, providing free medical and surgical procedures that bring health, hope, and training to people who would never be able to afford such services...*[7]

The ship was to be fitted out to become a floating hospital, the dream of Mercy Ships founder, Don Stephens, to operate off the coast of Africa. Our task was to renovate the entire ship, where she would be converted from a rail ferry into a floating hospital.

The ship was scheduled to arrive sometime after 1600 hours. We were supposed to be there in time to take photos of her arrival. However after a rushed trip, we arrived at Hebburn at 1615 only to find she had docked, and was already tied up. She had arrived in at 1430 and had beaten everyone there. When I arrived, the crew were trying to fit a gangway, but there wasn't a big enough crane to lift it into place. They had to rig a much shorter gangway, and due to a low spring tide, it was extremely steep. I remember climbing up it for the first time, behind Mae Palmer, Donovan's wife, who was about seven months pregnant, fearing that if she fell that she would probably fall right over the top of me.

My first impression of the ship was that she was huge. She towered above the dock and appeared impressively long. Most who see her for the first time have the same impression. She measured 152 metres long, 23.5 metres wide and contained eight decks. She was then classed as a 16,000-tonne ship. Later I discovered that was close to the size of Noah's Ark. She seemed to be well maintained and very tidy, with a black hull and white superstructure. There were very few cabins for a ship of its size, and they were mostly on deck seven with a few on deck two. Later we found out that the Danes who worked on her while she operated as a ferry were prohibited from using the cabins on deck two as they did not have a proper fire escape. There were three large restaurants and a coffee shop. Deck seven was reserved for the crew living quarters. The ship had two bridges, allowing it to sail in either direction. Nearly all the signs and instructions were in Danish, which made life a little difficult.

All of the crew who had sailed her over from Denmark were still on board, and we all had a meal of fish and chips together. They had been bought locally and were very greasy. Still, we all survived. There were 70 people for that first meal. I began my watchkeeping duties the next morning with a six-hour shift, and then later that night, another six hours.

The next day I was the first crew member to be signed on in the United Kingdom, by Captain Brian Sloane. I was to be on probation for three months to allow them to assess my abilities, and whether I would fit into the team. I later learned that this probationary period was a standard procedure for Mercy Ships and Youth With A Mission.

A lot of the original crew left that night, and within a few days there were only four of us left to look after this huge ship. There was: Geoff Morgan, our first officer; Juryanne Schute, an engineer and deck officer; Donovan, our project leader; and myself. Donovan then had to go back to Harpenden with his pregnant wife, Mae. We were shortly joined by our Chief Engineer Lubbert Veenstra, who had intended to sail over with the ship, but he had ended up in a Danish hospital because he had been working too hard and had upset his blood pressure. Regrettably he was not released from hospital in time to sail.

Initially my duties were serving as a watchkeeper and a plumber. While on watch we were to watch for fires, flooding or any other thing detrimental to the safety of the ship or crew. When I was on duty, Geoff asked me to thoroughly inspect every space on the ship, and to catalogue what was stored in the way of equipment. My prior experience working in Industrial Auctions proved invaluable, as I was able to identify much of the equipment onboard.

Next, the chief engineer, Lubbert, came to me and asked if I knew anything about vacuum toilets. I admitted that I had no experience with them, and neither had he. The ship had been docked for an extended period, and due to it having a vacuum toilet system, most of the toilets were not operating. We had a bit of a problem as all the instructions were in Danish, and neither of us could read them. In the end I asked if he had a parts diagram. He said he did, but it was all in Danish. I worked out how they operated by carefully following through the diagram.

So as the plumber, I was given the job of getting all of the toilets to work. My first job was to empty them all of their foul-smelling load. I was supplied with a wet and dry industrial vacuum cleaner and told to empty them. Eagerly determined to make a good impression with my hard work, I rushed about, gathered up a full load in the machine, and was charging along the passage to the elevator, when to my horror, I saw the tank starting to fall from the trolley I was pushing. I made a dive to catch it, but I was just too late. It tipped its foul, smelly load along the hallway outside the accommodation cabins. I certainly made an impression, but not quite the one that I intended. Two of the engineers who were still on board at that time, jumped out of the way as it spilt, laughed at me, then proceeded to help me to clean it up. I have never been able to live that incident down! I soon found a way to securely attach the tank to the trolley.

One incident that amused me was when the Chief's own toilet stopped working. He was determined to fix it himself. He had it in pieces many times, but still could not get it to work properly. Finally he went on leave for a short while, so I used my passkey to access his cabin and fixed it. The system was very old and it was quite hard to get parts for, so I recycled many parts from toilets that were not being used.

On April 10, 1999, we were joined by members of the DTS team who were unable to go to Kosovo. Donovan had invited them to join us instead. I went to the rail station and collected as much of their luggage as I could fit into my tiny Metro, a car made by BMC. Geoff also collected some luggage in Lubbert's equally small Suzuki. The DTS members caught the Metro, Newcastle's rail system, to Hebburn, and then walked to the ship. They were led by Chet Ingham and Chris Rainbow and they all stayed on board the ship. They engaged in all sorts of duties and were a great help to us on the ship, and a lot of fun to work with.

Near the end of their time with us, Donovan came to me and asked me to put on a Love Feast for the DTS team before they left. It involved cooking for thirty-six people. I had never cooked for this many people before, and was a bit anxious about taking it on but Donovan encouraged me, having heard of the dinners that I had cooked at Harpenden. I prepared a seafood cocktail for starters, a roast lamb and vegetables for the main course, and we bought a pavlova for dessert. The entrée was served in the engine room, and the main meal in one of the rear lounges, which gave me some problems in keeping it hot as it was quite a walk there. Then everyone was asked to don life-jackets and asked to assemble for a life-boat drill where the dessert was served. The Love Feast was a huge success and lots of fun.

The shipyard would occasionally need our berth to work on other ships. Our first shift to South Shields occurred on May 10, 1999, generating great excitement among the crew. First, the power and telephone lines were disconnected. The emergency generator was started to provide us with power for lights and the winches. Then the gangways were removed, the tugs hooked up, the smallest one to the stern and two larger tugs to the bow. We were towed stern-first, five miles downriver to our new berth. It was a time tinged with sadness as it meant we were out of the active shipyard, but it was better for the crew as we were closer to a nicer shopping centre and a quieter environment. Although the berth that we were towed to was in a closed shipyard, some work did continue while we were there.

The DTS were aboard for the move, but left us that day to return to the USA. We were very sad to see them go as they had been so obliging and helpful all the time with us. Prior to their departure, we had a simple communion together, and the crew sought a word from God which we shared with them. We were back to a crew of four again, and then a few days later there were just two of us looking after this huge ship for the rest of the week.

After my three-month probationary period as crew, I had not received any word from the management team. I went to Donovan and offered to leave at the end of the probation, but they told me they wanted me to stay on.

Not long after the *Dronning Ingrid* (now the *Africa Mercy*) arrived in Hebburn, First Officer Geoff Morgan asked all who were on board at the time to go away and ask God how He was going to provide for the ship. He did not want us to be focussed on Mammon (the god of greed and wealth). I went and prayed, and I had a vision, which is unusual for me.

I saw a large field of blackberry bushes, stretching for as far as the eye could see. The only thing was that they were very small bushes, not more than 18 inches high or more than two feet in diameter.

I was puzzled by this vision and asked God what he was showing me. He said to look closely at them, and I saw that they were covered in very succulent fruit. From this I came to the conclusion that there was great provision available just for the taking, but it would be from mostly small donors. The thoughts of this vision have remained with me, and, although I shared it at the time, I felt inclined not to act on it further. At the same time, Geoff Le Page, a marine crew assistant engineer, believed that Mercy Ships may transform many more vessels in that shipyard.

Shortly after this I was asked to help to arrange a lease for a flat for a new Crossroads team to use while they were with us. Crossroads was a Mercy Ships equivalent of the YWAM discipleship school (DTS). We managed to find a place in Hebburn that would accommodate about twelve people for a cost of £450 per month. We had to help find beds and other household items and furnish it for them.

There was great rejoicing on May 20, 1999, as Mae and Donovan welcomed a son into the world to add to their family of two daughters. Donovan, Mae and their children moved from Harpenden north to Hebburn at the end of June, and I drove their hired truck back to Harpenden. I had a few days of leave there, catching up with old friends.

Then I drove our new 17-seat bus back to the ship in Newcastle, with a load of stores for the office. The same day, June 28th, our first Crossroads team from Texas, USA, joined the ship for six weeks. They undertook cooking duties, and many of our other chores. They, like the DTS teams, were involved in outreach to many churches around Newcastle.

It was my pleasure to prepare a Love Feast for them at the conclusion of their outreach with us. Similar to the first team's departure, we had a prawn cocktail for starters followed by ham steaks, new potatoes and salad, with pavlova for dessert. They left us on the August 14th.

In between DTS visits, I filled in as Ship's Cook, cooking for up to 46 people. I frequently encountered difficulties with the domestic stove we used on board, as it seemed to have insufficient power. An American engineer who had come to help, rewired the ovens and managed to crash our whole power supply from shore. Later a different engineer found that it was only getting a 190 volt supply instead of the required 230 volts, which meant that both the oven and the stove elements failed to reach their normal heat.

During my night shift duties, I was instructed to remove the fittings from the aft bridge, as the plans were to demolish it and construct new living quarters in its place. The Superintendent was concerned I was getting too much done in a shift, and he thought this might upset the shipyard workers. The same thing happened when I was removing an unused toilet block too efficiently, but I preferred to keep busy or else the night shifts could drag.

City Church

I started attending City Church in Newcastle about this time. It was a lively spirit-filled group, meeting in a large building which they were turning into a church. The building had a large room which had formerly housed the turbines to generate the power for Newcastle's tram system. The plan was to use this area for their meetings. In the beginning we were divided between the top floor and the basement – both united by closed circuit TV as there was too big a congregation to fit in any one room! It was led by a team of elders, and had started when two cell groups had combined. The teaching was good, most of the time following a theme. The worship was excellent, and the whole service was very refreshing to me. Later the turbine hall was renovated and turned into the church meeting place. It accommodated about 400 people quite comfortably.

One time I went to City Church and during the service I noticed a particular young man attending, and felt that I had to speak to him after the service. I had never met him before, so I approached him and introduced myself. It was his first visit the church. It turned out that Tom was studying at South Shields Marine College to be a ships engineer, and he wanted to visit our ship. I invited him back and he had lunch with us and we gave him a tour of the ship. At the time, Tom had been struggling with the death of his youth pastor, and had been having trouble with a former landlady. We prayed together, and both issues were dealt with by God, and Tom found peace that only God can give. He became a regular visitor and later served onboard the *Anastasis* for a time.

Another time at the same church, one of the elders gave a prophesy in tongues. It was in a foreign language that he did not understand. At that time there were a number of Iranian Christians attending. One of the Iranian leaders jumped up excitedly and translated what had been said. He told us that it had been spoken in Fasi, and the prophesy was especially for the Iranians and also was for the whole church. As a congregation they welcomed us into their homes. They too had several visits to the ship.

Hebburn and South Shields

The original time estimate, for converting the ferry into a hospital ship, was initially one year, providing we had sufficient funds. To start with, very little appeared to be happening, but a lot of work was going on behind the scenes, including finalising plans and buoyancy calculations. As the berth was periodically needed by Cammell Laird, we were shifted to South Shields with tugs, the first of many relocations up and down the river. Although the Yard in South Shields was officially closed, a lot of removal work was done there, though none of the discarded steel could be removed from the ship until we were back at Hebburn.

Hebburn is a small town, not much bigger than a village. The local economy had previously relied on the shipbuilding and coal mining industries, but both had declined significantly by the time we arrived. There was a very small shopping centre, some industry, and was generally quite run down. Many locals had not ventured far beyond Newcastle, and some had never travelled more than five miles from their homes.

Jarrow and Hebburn were similar towns, though Jarrow had a larger shopping centre and further development of the retail district was planned. Both were about a mile from the ship. South Shields was a larger centre with more shops and more activities for the crew. The Metro rail system connected South Shields, Jarrow, Hebburn, and other stations, running all the way through to Newcastle and the airport. It was possible to change trains at Monument and take the northern loop to North Shields and other coastal areas.

At North Shields, we could catch a ferry across the Tyne River, back to South Shields. Later, another branch line was added to the Metro connected to Sunderland and beyond. A day pass cost less than £4 which allowed us to travel anywhere on the Metro, or use the buses within the limits of greater Newcastle.

Our second DTS team joined us on November 25, 1999, led by Chris Rainbow on her second visit, as well as Joette Valdez. The nine girls stayed in the flat that we had rented in Hebburn and the guys stayed in the Jarrow rectory. They were from the

Montana YWAM base in the USA. They quickly adapted to our routine and were very helpful, tackling every job with enthusiasm and cheerfulness.

I had great pleasure in taking a group of them for a day out to Hadrian's Wall, Carlisle and Gretna Green. Hadrian's Wall was built by the Romans to keep the Scots out of England, which the Romans occupied. Gretna Green was the first village in Scotland, and young people who eloped were able to be married there – by the blacksmith. The team left us on January 17, 2000. It was always sad to say goodbye to these teams.

Prayer Walking

One evening, shortly after we had arrived in Hebburn, Lubbert, our chief engineer, took me out to dinner in South Shields. It was a very cold and wet night. When we arrived there we noticed lots of girls walking in the streets, all dressed up in their best "Leopard Skins." The only problem was that they had not been able to catch very big leopards. We later found out that they were heading for the bars and clubs as it was free entry for the women on Thursday nights. Seeing all these scantily clad girls, some very young, brought me to tears. I think that it was God grieving for them. The picture of them remained in my heart for some time. I prayed about them, and from that I felt that God wanted me to prayer walk the market and the streets around the bars and clubs.

Upon visiting the South Shields Market, I was troubled by the sight of numerous very young, often unmarried mothers pushing prams. The market and surrounding area also had an abundance of pornographic material on display. During our time at South Shields, we started to prayer walk the streets of the town and the market. Initially we prayed through the streets in a spasmodic manner.

When Arlene Chase from the Texas Crossroads team joined us for a prayer walk, she likened the experience to "turning a furrow and ploughing a field" in preparation for seeding. This analogy led us to conclude that we should pray over the front and back of every house in the area. A number of people helped with this, from our own crew, as well as the crew from the *Anastasis* while they were docked in Newcastle. It seemed to have made a difference to the area. There seemed to be less pornographic videos available in the market, and families seemed more supportive of each other. The number of younger teenage mothers appeared to have decreased.

> *Finally, my brethren, be strong in the Lord, and in the power of his might. Put on the whole armour of God, that ye may be able to stand against the wiles of the devil. For we wrestle not against flesh and blood, but against principalities, against powers, against the rulers of the darkness of this world, against spiritual wickedness in high places. Wherefore take unto you the whole armour of God, that ye may be able to withstand in the evil day, and having done all, to stand.* (Ephesians 6:10-13 KJV)

Prayer walking requires good preparation, I found this out the hard way. I took a team out prayer walking, without any preparation, and the next day had a group of people in serious trouble. We had forgotten to prepare by putting on the full armour of God, and at the finish to ask God for His cleansing by the Blood of Jesus. We gathered together and asked God to forgive us and to set us free from the bondage of the evil one, which He graciously did. We eventually covered an area from the river to the coast and from South Shields to Tyne Dock. It took us nearly three years to complete.

Hebburn

On February 29, 2000, the *Dronning Ingrid* was relocated from South Shields back up to Hebburn late in the night. As soon as the ship was back in the original yard, Cammell Laird erected scaffolding around the funnel and repainted it in our new colours. They made a steel Mercy Ships logo and attached and painted it.

Around this time, Les and Sylvia Paul gave their notice of resignation. For several months, they had handled the ship's bookkeeping and galley operations. Additionally, Les served as the Crew Services Manager. The decision was then made for me to assume the bookkeeper responsibilities. As this was my first time keeping books on a computer, despite my familiarity with double-entry bookkeeping, I needed a crash course to learn the necessary computer skills. Les and Sylvia left us in March of 2000. Amy Crawford, the accountant overseeing our project based in Stevenage, travelled from Harpenden to manage the transition from Les and Sylvia to me.

A date was set for officially renaming the ship. I was given the job of arranging the purchase of T-shirts and fleeces for the crew for the renaming ceremony. This involved finding a manufacturer and working out how to best use the new Mercy Ships logo on the garments. The majority of the order was for polo shirts, but I put in a special request for the logo on a jersey. Only three jerseys were embroidered with the Mercy Ships logo, and to this day these are my prized wardrobe items. As the time for the ceremony grew closer, I spent hours racing around finding seats to accommodate the cast of thousands that were invited to the event.

Our visitors came from across the country and around the world. Our distinguished guests included Ann Gloag of the Balcraig Foundation, Don Stephens, the founder and president of Mercy Ships, and Dame Norma Major. Other VIPs included Brian Sloane, Jim Patterson, Donovan Palmer and numerous representatives from the YWAM leadership teams across the globe, as well as staff members from our Stevenage office.

With great pomp and ceremony, the ship was renamed the *Africa Mercy* on April 4th, 2000. Formalities were conducted by the wife of former Prime Minister Sir John Major, Dame Norma Major. She had been awarded her title in recognition of her distinguished charity work, making her the most appropriate person to preside over our celebration.

> *"Dame Norma Major to Christen New Mercy Ship!" read the headline. From around the world, we traveled to the Newcastle shipyard on the River Tyne to stand at the edge of a dock. The Naming Ceremony of the* Africa Mercy, *the newest member of the Mercy Ships fleet, had just begun. "I am delighted to be standing here with you as we celebrate the many voyages of hope and healing that lie ahead. It now gives me great pleasure to name this ship the* Africa Mercy. *May God bless her, and all who sail on her," said Dame Norma Major, wife of former British Prime Minister John Major. Then she shot a champagne bottle from a launcher, the bottle smashed against the side of the ship, and the master of ceremonies of the shipyard led the crowd in three cheers as a bagpipe band began to play. Why the bagpipes? In honor of Ann Gloag, the Scottish woman who had made the day possible.*[8]

Work on the newly renamed ship continued, and Cammell Laird removed a large amount of steel and fittings that were not required. The rail deck was originally very high to allow for trains and so there was room to install an additional deck above the existing rail deck. The crew were very involved in removing and storing the fittings from the ship to give the yard better access for the renovations.

We were later shifted further up the river to a berth at the old Hawthorne Leslie yard. It was right on a bend in the river, and our officers had voiced their concern that it was not a secure berth for our size of ship. This was later proved correct, when, during a force 10 gale, the pontoons that were holding us clear of the berth collapsed and we were blown aground. So on December 1st, tugs were called to get us afloat. This was accomplished with some difficulty, the tug captain saying that anything could be moved with 80% power, but they had to use slightly more to get us unstuck. They spent the next 24 hours holding us, until another temporary berth had been arranged back at South Shields. Shortly afterwards we were again shifted back to Hebburn to a more secure berth, where the new deck was finally completed.

We were supported in prayer by the Lydia group, who on several occasions had come and spent time praying on the ship. Lydia is an interdenominational fellowship of ladies who meet together in small groups uniting in prayer, and is based on the women of the Bible. We really appreciated their support.

I went back to New Zealand on my annual leave for a month at the end of August 2000, and when I came back at the end of September the ship was back at Hebburn, and work had started in earnest.

Tribulation

On the 4th of May, 2000, I got a message saying that my house in New Zealand had burnt down during the night, and that the tenants had only got out with the clothes that they were wearing. Five fire engines from Papakura and Manurewa, located 20 minutes away, responded to the blaze, but strangely, the Hūnua fire crew, who were only five kilometres away, did not.

Photos were emailed to me that day, and there was nothing left except part of the brick walls. Initially I was devastated, and in my cabin, I shed a few tears, but after a few minutes a thought popped into my mind, "But you dedicated it to Me!" Suddenly I remembered that I had dedicated the house to God in 1990, so I was able to put it back in His hands, and I immediately had peace. That peace lasted through an investigation into the cause of the fire by the police and throughout the rebuilding process. It was later suggested that the tenants had burnt it down deliberately to get insurance on their contents. My fellow crew members were amazed at my lack of stress over the news, but I had complete peace after I put it in God's hands.

Whilst overseas, I had given power of attorney to my friend Peter, who had let me know about the fire. I offered to return to New Zealand to oversee everything, but Peter said that he would see to everything, as his ministry in support of me. Peter and Jenni were absolutely wonderful, helping to work out a better design for the house while keeping it under the same roof area. They chose all the colours, carpets and vinyl, and I was able to view all their hard work when I returned for a visit in September. Further to this, their boys helped me to clean up around the section and put in new drainage. As I got off the plane in Auckland, I was greeted by Peter with the words, "God really looks after you, doesn't He?" I must agree with him. I feel that God has really blessed me since I have been obedient to Him. That is not to say though that my life has been plain sailing – far from it. There have been many times that I have been tested, but I have always been sure that He has been right beside me through all those testing times.

When I had been home the year before, I had felt that Peter and Jenni had been getting tired of looking after my affairs, and I was wondering who could replace them if it became too much. But they had come to visit the ship in England, and were so impressed with what we were doing, and from that visit they felt that it was their way of supporting me.

Both YWAM and Mercy Ships have a culture of compassionate care for crew members who may be facing difficult personal circumstances. One example of this was a family, who had their house trashed by tenants while they were away, and needed to do considerable refurbishment. A collection was taken up among our small crew and £1,400 was raised to donate towards their costs.

The UK tax laws are quite complex, and I felt that I needed to check out my tax position with the UK Tax office, as I had not registered with them while living in Britain, and I was a little concerned that I should have done so previously. I visited the local tax office and they were so helpful. I explained my situation to them, how all my income came from New Zealand and was brought in by Visa Card, and I did not have a bank account in this country. As New Zealand has reciprocal tax arrangements, I found that I did not even have to file a tax return in the UK. As a footnote, I have nearly always found the tax offices to be helpful if you approach them directly.

In early March 2001, our crew renovations team started to tear out our shower bases so that the floors could be repaired and the bases resurfaced. This meant that we were without our showers and toilets for up to two weeks, although we had access to other showers some distance away. This was among the many small discomforts. At one time it was very cold and we didn't have heating as it wasn't working for some reason. One of the girls felt the cold so much that she ran her hot shower all night to warm the cabin up a bit. The Chief Engineer was not at all pleased. We often had power cuts and water shortages, most of which were dealt with quite quickly.

On April 11, 2001, we heard that Cammell Laird had ceased trading on the Stock Exchange due to financial problems. As they were doing our construction work, we were rather concerned. They went into receivership the next day, but continued to work on the ship until early June. This prompted the crew to spend a lot more time in prayer. Just before the collapse we had been getting rather complacent in our relationship with God. We certainly became much more focussed on our relationship with Him from then on.

The yard had the new alternators for the ship ready to lower into place on April 28, 2001. They weighed 12.5 tonnes each and had to be manoeuvred carefully into a very restricted place. They were loaded onto the deck of the ship and a few days later, holes were cut through the decks to allow them to be lowered into the engine room. This was the last job that Cammell Laird did for us. We were treated very well by Cammell Laird, who did not charge us for berths all of the time they were working on the ship.

So then, the hunt was on for another company to complete the work. Several firms registered their interest to take over the contract, and we had lots of people coming onboard to make assessments of the remaining work.

We had an intriguing man join the ship as our Captain. He had obviously had some encounter with the Lord, but we did not know how. A day or so later he took me aside and confided in me. He shared the heartbreaking story of his young son, who had suddenly passed away while at school, from a rare heart disorder. They were devastated, but he described how a day or so later he was standing by the child's swing when he felt God's presence and an incredible sense of peace. Sometime after joining our crew, he quietly gave his heart to the Lord during one of our meetings, later sharing this with me.

On May 5, 2001, we were shifted back to South Shields to allow the Shipyard to finish some of the other work that they were doing.

At one point, the Cole family crew, including Andy, the Second Engineer, and Brenda, the Personnel Manager, fell ill. Frank van Eck suggested that we visit their home and hold a worship service together. When we arrived, the Coles seemed listless and lacking their usual energy. Frank led the service, and I sang along as best I could, despite my well-known inability to carry a tune. Gradually, the family joined in the songs of praise, and to our delight, they all recovered quickly.

Later in May, Captain Ben Woolley invited me to stay with him. As we were en-route, Ben got a phone call to say that his wife Anna had suffered a heart attack. Though I offered to go back to the ship, Ben insisted on me continuing with him. The situation was quite serious and she had been admitted to hospital. Their oldest son had performed mouth-to-mouth resuscitation to keep her alive. While Ben focused on Anna's care, I was able to comfort the rest of the family. Fortunately Anna made a full recovery and was able to return to her part-time job.

Among all the work on the ship, moves up and down the river, and special fellowship times, I have a cherished memory of attending the wedding of Radcliffe Lewis and Paula Gower on June 30, 2001. Radcliffe, one of our engineers, and Paula, a nurse at South Shields Hospital, had both been involved with Mercy Ships for some time. Radcliffe is Nigerian, while Paula is English.

One day I went to the Metro to catch a train to church. I had just missed the first one and had to wait 20 minutes for the next. As I waited, a young lady came and stood just outside the station smoking vigorously and appearing very agitated. I felt God prompting me to talk to her, but in my usual hesitation I procrastinated, worried she would see me as an intrusive old man, and not want to talk to me. God kept prodding me and finally I mustered the courage to ask if she was alright.

She explained she was late for work and was frightened that she would lose her job. Then she told me that she worked at the markets as a cleaner, one of the lowest paid jobs, and that she worked five hours per day or less. She told me that she was 22 and had a five-year-old and a one-year-old child, plus a live-in boyfriend who was unemployed, and that she was the sole provider for the family. Her situation was overwhelming and she had been considering suicide as a way out. As the train arrived, I asked if I could sit beside her on the way into Newcastle. She agreed, and after further discussion she allowed me to pray for her. I gave her my mobile phone number and encouraged her to ring at any hour and I would connect her with one of the ladies on the ship to talk to her. Though she never called, I later saw her and she appeared a lot happier and more settled. I also asked other people on the ship to pray for her. I have often wondered what became of her.

In 2001 a devastating outbreak of Foot and Mouth disease struck Northumbria, eventually spreading across the United Kingdom. It was very disheartening to witness so many fires burning all the animals that were culled in an attempt to stop the spread of the disease. As a farmer myself, I deeply sympathised with those affected. Earlier, I had been invited to visit a farm that belonged to one of our Church members. I had a lovely day visiting their place and comparing farming practices to my own experiences in New Zealand. Sadly, their stock too, were later condemned. I was very upset knowing how much effort had been put into developing their animals. The outbreak lasted 221 days and 6.45 million animals were culled.

In mid-July we had the first meeting with a company called MSC, who eventually signed a letter of intent to build the cabins and offices. On the very next day they started needle gunning (extremely noisy paint and rust removal) on the deck above our offices and it was impossible to work with the noise. This carried on for a few afternoons and was quite disruptive, so we all found jobs to do in other parts of the ship or ashore.

I was taken to Beamish Museum near Durham one day and it was an incredible place! We spent the whole day there, and wished we had more time to explore. The active displays, the people dressed in period costume who were well-versed in what it would have been like to have lived in those times. I later visited several more times, taking others to see it. I was able to get a greater appreciation of all the work that had gone into establishing it. They had an incredible array of historic artefacts, including old steam trains, trams, and a whole village.

While we were at South Shields some of us made friends with the crew of the tug boats, which resulted in many of us being invited to go on board the tugs while they were working.

We got a lot of enjoyment out of it as well as being able to talk to the crews about what we were doing and why. These experiences gave us a better understanding and appreciation of the work of the tugs and their hardworking crews.

In July a delightful Scottish couple, John and Bernadette Graham, arrived on the ship. John was meant to fill in as Chief Engineer and Bernadette was going to help me in the accounts department. Everything was progressing smoothly – I was training Bernadette and they had fitted well in with the crew. However we got news that the *Anastasis* was desperately short of a Chief Engineer, so they were both spirited away to the *Anastasis*. I was very upset as I desperately needed help. But such is the reality of working for any Christian organisation. Regrettably, I never did get an assistant in the accounts department.

August 2001 marked the arrival of the first of the ship's new Landrover Defenders. They are very nice four-wheel-drive vehicle, and reminded me of the early days of the ship in Newcastle, when we had only one car, a Metro. It was tiny and I remembered three people crammed into it and then the week's groceries for 27 crew packed in around them. Later we were fortunate to be donated the money to purchase a Vauxhall Station Wagon (Estate Car) and a Mini Bus that could carry 17 people. Since then we have been donated several cars, and a Camper Van for crew recreation. Another blessing to us was that a Scottish mechanic, Stan Lamb, offered his services for free, to inspect and do any repairs required. Later he was very helpful in assisting to find private cars for many of the crew.

Our leaders had been negotiating with a shipyard on the other side of the river to complete the ship's renovation. However on September 3rd, we learned that the AMP shipbuilding berth was unavailable – the river needed dredging to provide adequate depth, and that local environmental issues prevented this dredging. We were advised that we would probably need to move away from the Tyne River and find another location. Most of the crew were stunned and quite concerned. Fortunately AMP later bought the old Cammell Laird yard and they were able to continue the work on our ship.

We were also stunned on 11th of September to see on the news the two planes crashing into the World Trade Centre in New York. This was very tough on our American crew, especially for one woman whose father was a pilot for American Airlines, the company whose planes had been hijacked. She knew that he was flying that day, and she could not raise him on his cell phone or contact her family. Fortunately she learned he was safe. He and his wife later became involved in counselling the other airline crews affected by the tragedy.

We also learned that one of our crew's families, who were on their way to do a Crossroads Course in Texas, could not enter USA airspace due to this event. They were forced to land in Newfoundland, where they were stranded for several days. They and many other families were accommodated by local churches. This tragic incident impacted air travel worldwide.

On September 21st, I finally received my new UK visa, to my great relief. I had been concerned they might deny it, as most of my New Zealand income had dried up after my tenants vacated without notice, and it had been difficult to find replacement tenants. The next day I tried to book tickets to fly home, but all the planes were booked solid to the end of January. It seemed many people had booked to fly to the southern hemisphere after the devastating events of September 11.

After spending six hours at various travel agents, I finally secured a ticket to fly just four days later – much sooner than

I had originally intended to travel. Then there was a big rush to get everything in order before my departure. I spent some time helping my colleague, Nathan Ward, with the day-to-day account management. I then left the ship on September 26, 2001 for my three months' leave of absence, and returned home to New Zealand.

After returning from my leave, I arrived back to find more changes in the crew aboard the ship. Initially I felt quite unsettled and wondering what I was doing here until God reminded me about my prayer for my visa. I had prayed that God would block my visa if I was not supposed to be here, but that He would grant it, despite my income being very poor at the time of the application. Another source of comfort for me settling back into my life there was an American couple, Jim and Susan Martin, who joined us as crew. They ministered to me significantly, and they also restarted a regular Prayer group meeting.

Ship-based Schools

In the middle of 2001 Larry and Barbara Hurt joined our team, with plans to establish the first onboard *Africa Mercy* Discipleship Training School. They brought their staff along as well. However, they discovered that hosting the school on the ship would exceed our insurance limits for the number of people on board. Needing to find an alternative, they started to investigate where they could accommodate both the students and staff. Fortunately, South Shields Marine College generously offered their facilities during the early part of the New Year. The team also found a nearby church, St Michaels, to serve as a classroom. Overall, this worked out well and they were able to successfully accommodate the training school off the ship, allowing the programme to go ahead as planned.

In January 2002 Larry and Barb started the first school. The school featured a diverse array of speakers, and students spent two afternoons per week helping with tasks around the ship. Sixteen students from around the world attended the three-month school programme, before travelling to the *Anastasis* in The Gambia, West Africa, for their outreach and practical experience. During the afternoons, the students helped on the ship with various duties.

As a crew, we greatly enjoyed having the students on board, and found them to be very helpful completing many tasks that we hadn't time to do ourselves. One of the things that I loved most about having the schools associated with us, was witnessing the spiritual growth and development of the students throughout the programme.

In March 2002 I was given a small 1986 Vauxhall Nova, by some people in Scotland. Dave Roderick drove it down for me, since I still need to get my British driver's license. I eventually managed to exchange my New Zealand driving licence for a British one.

The car had originally been obtained for another crew member, but by the time it was ready, he had already been given another car. It was offered to me, but I was unsure about accepting it, since my income was limited at that time. After praying about it, I felt God say that He would provide for my needs. Soon after, Frank van Eck told me he believed that God would supply what I needed to run the car. Accepting the gift, I added other crew members to the insurance policy so that they could use it as well. I affectionately called it "a matchbox on wheels."

While visiting a friend in Dorset, he suggested I take my car to his local garage for a check-up and service. I could just afford the service, but the garage then found an additional, costly issue. Though I was concerned this would exceed my budget, I decided to trust that God would provide. When I inquired about the total repair cost, I was surprised and delighted to learn it had already been paid for. God had indeed provided for the unexpected car maintenance expenses.

Sometime later I was on my way home from the Keswick Convention, when the exhaust pipe broke. The car was very noisy. I went to the local garage and asked for a quote. It was for £120 so I reluctantly agreed to go ahead. When it was finished, I went to pay for it and the proprietor questioned me to find out if it was my own car, when I said it was, he only charged me for the parts and not the labour. It cost me £60 and he told me that as I had introduced Mercy Ships to his garage, he wanted to say thank you. I managed to give some of the money that I had saved to another crew member who had an unexpected expense on her car.

2003 *Discipleship Training School*

Larry and Barb returned in late 2002 to prepare for the next Discipleship Training School (DTS). Unfortunately some of their previous leaders decided not to participate, however, several students from the previous year's course stepped up to help. They managed to assemble a group of 28 students.

They then received some troubling news. South Shields College notified them that the accommodation they had used the prior year was not available. This was a setback as they had hoped to use the same facilities again. Faced with this challenge, Larry and Barb engaged in fervent prayer, determined to find suitable housing for the 30 students and eight staff members.

Despite doors seemingly closing at every turn, they persisted, keeping their focus on God. This period of uncertainty lasted nearly two weeks and was quite stressful, but they felt the Lord's presence guiding them. During this time, they exhausted every idea to secure appropriate housing, knowing this was critical to hosting the DTS lectures.

After initially searching in Newcastle, Hexham, Sunderland, and Durham, they eventually found a promising option in the Scottish Borders. This location met all their needs, including space for lectures, except that it was too far from the ship – about 70 miles away. However, it could still work well, as it could accommodate all the staff and students, had good meeting facilities, and the proprietor was a personal friend of Dame Ann Gloag, the woman who had purchased the ship for them. This was a good backup plan in case they couldn't find a closer option.

Another opportunity arose in South Shields through a lady named Carol who they had no previous connection with, but as soon as she heard about their mission, she wanted to help in any way that she could. Carol went to work on their behalf and arranged for the use of three guest houses at a much-reduced rate which was within their financial capabilities. There was much anxiety, but as they prayed about it, the group felt confident that it was the right place to be. With Carol's help, they were able to make the necessary arrangements.

That was nowhere near the end of their problems. Late on the night of December 28th, Barb received a call from Larry to say that the car had broken down in Jarrow, and he needed a ride home. She got out of bed and went to collect him. Meanwhile, the other car had also broken down. Larry was able to fix that one, but the first car had to be towed to the garage where it was repaired on Monday for a very reasonable price.

On the same day they managed to get hold of St Michaels

Church, but found to their dismay that the church was unavailable for the lectures due to an ongoing construction project. This was especially devastating as they had developed a close relationship with the church the previous year.

Immediately after receiving this disappointing news, they contacted the Peoples Mission Church, which was conveniently located in the area near the student guest houses. Interestingly, several weeks earlier, while prayer walking in that area, we had felt led by God to pray around that very church seven times. We could see God's hand in the arrangements, as the People's Mission Church was now available to host the lectures

The DTS team immediately contacted one of the elders of the Peoples Mission Church, who was very receptive to the idea. This elder then phoned the other church elders and then invited Larry and Barb to meet with them at 6.15pm, indicating the church's willingness to help in any way possible. The DTS team offered to pay for the heating and any other costs incurred, but the church believed that God would provide for those expenses. In fact, the church considered it a privilege that the DTS had asked to use their facilities.

Amazed at how rapidly the problems had been resolved, Larry and Barb attributed it all to God's divine hand. In the past, organising such events had been trying, but this time the facilities were excellent, conveniently located near the guest houses and eliminated the need to find transport. They left the meeting praising God, convinced it was His handiwork, all coming together in just a few hours.

This year, the organisation faced numerous setbacks, including staff changes, location changes, and vehicle problems. Yet, through our faithfulness to God, these challenges were quickly overcome. Interestingly, in prior years, God had directed the

South Shields Prayer walkers to intercede around the Peoples Mission church on multiple occasions.

Trust in the Lord with all your heart, and lean not on your own understanding. Acknowledge Him in all your ways and He will make your paths straight. (Adapted from Proverbs 3:5-6)

One day, I was speaking to Kerri-Anne, a local who was assisting on the ship, and asking her about God's call on her life. She confided she felt called to attend a Discipleship Training School (DTS) in Perth, Australia, but lacked necessary funds. I questioned why she was hesitant to be obedient to God's leading. Encouraging her, I suggested that if it was truly God's plan, He would provide the means, and suggested that she write to the YWAM base in Perth and enquire about it. She did this, but when she got the information back she started to worry. Sensing God's guidance, I suggested that she read Isaiah 43: 1-7 and Proverbs 3:5-6.

After applying and being accepted to the YWAM programme in Perth, Australia, Kerri-Ann faced a series of challenges. With the DTS programme starting soon, she needed to get a new passport, a visa to get into Australia, an airline ticket and raise enough funds to cover the course costs. At each step there were delays, and her faith was seriously tested, but I and many others kept encouraging and praying with her.

She could not book her air ticket until she received her passport and visa, and airline seats to Perth were in high demand. Eventually, funds arrived just in time for each need, and after an agonising wait, she received her visa to enter Australia. Finally, when she was ready to book her airline ticket, she discovered the seat that she was hoping for had been sold, but luckily she found another less expensive seat on an earlier flight. Through faith in God, determination and with prayer support, she overcame the logistical hurdles and made it to the YWAM programme in Australia.

When I returned from one of my trips to New Zealand, accommodation at the time was quite limited on the ship so I was asked to share a cabin with one of the other crew members. He disliked sharing his cabin. Trying to be considerate, I made the mistake of asking him to kick the bottom of my bunk if I snored. Sure enough, I was frequently woken by kicks throughout the night.

One night, as I lay awake listening to him snore, he let out an extra-large snore that woke him up. To my amusement, he immediately kicked on the bottom of my bunk! I nearly fell out as I laughed so hard.

Around this time, I was asked to help carry some heavy equipment up the gangway. As I stepped onto the bottom of the gangway, the person behind pushed at the wrong time, throwing all the weight onto my ankle, spraining it. It caused me a lot of problem climbing in and out of my bunk, so I asked if I could be transferred into the dormitory where I did not need to climb into a bunk. Fortunately my request was granted, and the boys in there did not complain about my snoring!

Make your own commitment

While staying in the dormitory, I shared it with a young Norwegian lad who had done a DTS course in his home country. However, his leaders had not allowed him to go on outreach with the team, so he had been sent to us instead. This decision had caused him to feel hurt, and I spent considerable time ministering to him. Later, I was given my own cabin and he frequently visited and asked questions. He often seemed down and discouraged, so we would talk and pray together. Though he would usually leave in a much happier frame of mind, in a few days he would return, just as despondent as before. This kept puzzling me, so I continued to ask God about it.

One day the lad came to visit, and I felt God prompting me to "ask him questions." I was puzzled about what to ask, until I recalled a time when, doubting my ability to hear God, a friend's questioning revealed that God had been speaking to me all along. So I asked the lad how he had become a Christian. He said he had always been one. When I asked what he meant by that, he said that his parents were Christians. I gently suggested that he needed to make his own personal commitment to Christ. I advised that he go and pray about it, also giving him two copies of the "sinner's prayer" from *The Word for Today*, recommending that if he prayed the "sinner's prayer," he should share this with two other people. The next morning he came rushing up to me to say that he had done it!

A few weeks later I was talking to a young Scottish engineer after dinner. He expressed how difficult it was for someone whose job involves proving everything, to believe in Christ, as this takes a step of faith. As we continued talking, I could see that God was touching his heart. However, I felt that God did not want me to push the matter further, so I let it go.

The next day the Norwegian lad excitedly told me that he had led the engineer to the Lord. Later, the two of them spent time together serving on one of the other ships. Eventually the engineer became a Presbyterian minister in Edinburgh, UK, conducting services in both English and Cantonese.

In May 2003 it was time for my furlough (leave of absence),

so I went home to New Zealand. My youngest daughter had been unwell, and although the diagnosis was uncertain, it was suspected to be chronic fatigue syndrome.

Upon arriving in Christchurch I found Joanne struggling with basic tasks due to a lack of energy. Determined to do as much as she could, she asked me to bring the washing out to the clothesline so she could hang it herself. As I watched, she would hang two items on the line and then rest until she had enough energy to continue. Her husband, David, had been staying home from work to care for her and their children. With me assisting with some duties, David was able to return to his job and maintain his employment.

For two weeks, I prayed daily in my room for Joanne's healing. One day, I felt that God wanted me to lay hands on her and pray for her recovery. After I did so, Joanne returned to her household chores, and I attributed this to God's healing power. I then expressed concern that she was doing too much, and in trying to protect her, she became irritated with me.

After deciding to go home, and do some more work on my house in South Auckland, I received a phone call from her two weeks later. She and her youngest son Sam had just spent two nights in hospital. Sam had borrowed a skateboard and was trying it out on the footpath outside their home when he collided with a power pole and broke his leg in two places. He was in hip to toe plaster and Joanne had to carry her nine-year-old son everywhere.

Instead of seeking God's guidance, or asking Joanne, I flew back to Christchurch thinking she would need my help. However, I soon realised I was only getting in the way of my very independent daughter, so I hired a car and drove to visit some friends near Invercargill. I had a good time with them and was even asked to preach at their church. During this visit, they asked me if I was still expecting to rejoin the ship. I felt confident that I was supposed to return for another year, but beyond that I remained unsure and would continue to seek God's will.

Leaving New Zealand to return to the UK on my way back to the ship, I stopped in Australia and stayed with some good friends in Sydney. They had often helped me focus on God for answers, but this time I left a bit disappointed that God had not spoken to me about my future.

My next stop was Singapore, where my friends James and Belinda Ginns were living. James greeted me at the airport and said, "Your ten years must be just about up!" When I asked him what he meant, he reminded me that when I was working with him in Hong Kong, I had felt God had called me out of New Zealand for ten years. This resonated with me, and after returning to the ship, God later confirmed it through others.

South Shields House

On arrival back in Newcastle I found that all of the crew had been removed from the ship as it had been shifted to another shipyard on the other side of the river. Consequently they were accommodated in flats and boarding houses over a wide area. I was sent to a boarding house in South Shields, and the day after I arrived there was asked to take over the cooking for up to 18 people. In addition to this, I was also asked to do all the food purchasing for the other houses.

At that time there was a crew of about 40 people plus locals who were helping on the ship. I managed to make contact with some wholesalers and to re-establish relationship with the green grocers in an attempt to keep our costs down. Keeping everyone happy was very challenging. Our budget at that time was £2, 75p (about NZ$5) per day per crew member, and quite achievable.

In our South Shields house, we hosted a diverse group of 13 people from nine different nationalities, each with their own unique food preferences. The Africans liked rice for every meal, while the British preferred potatoes over rice, and many Americans desired pasta. Attempting to balance the meals over the week failed to satisfy everyone's individual tastes and dietary needs. Some refused to eat cheese or fish, while others had restrictions on salt and sugar intake.

Eventually I was appointed House Coordinator. It meant I was responsible for running the house and sorting out various grievances. There were all sorts of complaints, from dirty toilets to missing money, and people not doing their share of the chores.

Rather than establishing a list of rules, I wanted the crew to take personal responsibility for organising and maintaining the household. Though I frequently received complaints, I would first pray about the issues before investigating further. If the complaint was directed at a specific individual, I instructed the complainant to address the matter privately with that person. If the private discussion failed to resolve the problem, I asked both parties to meet with me, at which point the issue was generally settled amicably.

One day, a crew member came to me with a specific complaint. I told him I would pray about it and get back to him. He became very upset, saying I always prayed but never took action. I explained that when I didn't pray, I made poor decisions. Upset, he stormed out into the snow and sleet for an hour.

When he returned, the crew member apologised, saying God had spoken to him and that my approach was the right thing. I later discovered the person he had accused was not actually the culprit – it was one of the crew member's friends instead. This person felt repentant after hearing a story I shared at a meeting, and they subsequently confessed. From that point on, they took their responsibilities more seriously.

One day I went to the Shore office about the accounts, and the leaders were having a meeting. When I got there, they were all arguing heatedly. I laughed at them and suggested that the Devil had them by the tail. They all glared at me. I reminded them that our battle is not against flesh and blood but against the spirits of this dark world (Ephesians 6). I suggested that they bind the Devil and ask God to bring them into unity, which they did. Everything went smoothly from then on.

We were all invited to a wedding in Edinburgh of two of our crew members. I offered a ride up there to one of our crew members. He was a bit notorious at letting other people pay for him without making any effort to help out himself. He was a bit put out that I was not staying at the boarding house as I had arranged private accommodation.

Despite this, we enjoyed the wedding and had a great time. On the way up, I had paid for his lunch and all the fuel, leaving me feeling a little resentful by the time we headed back. I was going to skip lunch myself rather than ask him to pay, but fortunately, I felt compelled to do the right thing. So, albeit a bit begrudgingly, I ended up buying him lunch as well.

After the drive back, he told me he wanted to attend an ex-crew member's wedding in the States, but couldn't afford the trip. I suggested he try blessing others with his funds for a month and see what happened. He did, and the funds came in for the wedding. Sadly, he reverted to his old ways, and still struggles financially.

I have always liked the following verse:

> *Give, and it will be given to you: good measure, pressed down, shaken together, and running over...* (Luke 6:38)

As I write this, I'm listening to the song "Give Thanks with a Grateful Heart." In my own life, I've found that when funds are short, giving to someone else often results in the needed money arriving. I'm yet to see a time when this hasn't happened.

Setting an Example

Managing a ship-based operation while still connected to shore often presents challenges in the chain of command. Some leaders navigate these differences effectively, while others struggle. Operation Mobilisation faced similar problems in its early days.

On a ship, the deck and engineering officers hold absolute authority, as they are trained to oversee the vessel and crew. The operational management must defer to the marine officers when it comes to ship and personnel safety. However, the operational team maintains control over deployment locations, accounting, fundraising, and the deployment of crew ashore. I observed that if the marine or operations side disobeys the rules of their environment, they quickly lose the respect and authority of those under their command. It is crucial that there is a full understanding and alignment of each role and its boundaries.

With work to do on the ship, the team needed to follow marine management, and while on shore, operational management. My favourite quote that we heard often from officer Geoff Morgan was, "Open your eyes, see where a job needs doing, and step in and do it."

Living in a large household, we all had to work together and share the household chores. Frustrated by some housemates neglecting their duties, which I was largely responsible for coordinating, I decided to rewrite my job description in a tongue-in-cheek manner. I then presented this to each housemate individually, silently observing as they read it.

I outlined how some house members were leaving all the work to others. Finally I added the following as a lesson: Jesus was the Servant King; He washed the disciples' feet. He constantly served others. Can we do any less? If we do not do our share, we cause others to sin, by grumbling and complaining.

> *If anyone causes one of these little ones to lose faith, it would be better for him to have been thrown into the sea with a large millstone around his neck...* (Adapted from Matthew 18:6)

The result was from that point on I no longer had trouble with all house members doing chores and, in fact, they were falling over themselves to do the jobs around the house.

A visitor
In 2003 my middle daughter, Sandy, came for a visit to see me. I picked her up from the airport in my "matchbox on wheels" and we drove out to the ship in the dockyard. Like me, she was impressed with the size of the ship and I showed her around all of the areas of the ship in its varying stages of renovation. We went down into the engine room where I showed her one of my current tasks. All of the nameplates for various items on the ship required translation from Danish into English. The translation caused no problems, but I cannot say the same about the "damn labelling machine" that made the name plates. The manual was one and a half inches thick, which I duly read and learnt nothing! So after much re-reading, trial and error, I man-

aged to summarise the instructions into a couple of pages – and I later heard those pages were invaluable and stayed in use for a long time.

I arranged a couple of days off and we went on a mini tour in the flying matchbox, and visited the northern English and Scottish towns that she wanted to see. I took her on my guided tour of Hadrian's Wall and the other local tourist spots, then we headed to Edinburgh, Perth, Hamilton and Bannockburn, which matched names of places she has lived in the Southern Hemisphere. She was amazed at the price of fuel, to fill up the tiny tank of the Vauxhill Viva at that time was more than double the cost of filling her six-cylinder Mitsubishi back in Australia.

Upon returning to the UK from my furlough in New Zealand, I was assigned to house duties overseeing the crew, leaving me with less work on the ship. The Operations Manager, who had originally placed me in the accounting department with a £70 million budget, had now put me in charge of the boarding house instead of my preferred position on the ship. After all of my other experiences, I didn't feel that this would be my calling for much longer.

The ship wouldn't be completed for another 18 months. I would have loved to sail on its maiden journey as a newly refitted floating hospital. However, without marine or medical expertise, this was not a realistic possibility for me.

By early 2004 I had been away from home on mission work abroad for a decade, and at 66 years old, I was looking forward to the tranquility of my farm. James Ginn had previously reminded me of this "ten-year period" in God's service, so I felt my time in England drawing to a close. I am incredibly grateful that while there, I experienced the amazing leadership of four gentlemen in particular, Donovan Palmer, Ben Woolley, Geoff

Morgan and Ken Hudson. They are all fondly remembered and will always have a special place in my heart and prayers.

NINE
FULL CIRCLE
RETURNING HOME

My Son, Be Wise
Do not boast about tomorrow,
For you do not know what a day may bring forth.
Let another man praise you, and not your own mouth...
(Proverbs 27:1-2a)

After I came back to New Zealand at the start of 2004, I was hesitant to return to the church that had sent me out as a missionary. It had been through a time of uncertainty. The minister who had been with the church for many years, had retired because of his age. The assistant pastor, Bruce, had resigned to form a new church two years before the minister retired.

Many of the elders and parishioners followed him, causing some bitterness in the remaining congregation. It was interesting to note that this new church grew bigger under his leadership and attracted an entirely different congregation.

While serving in Hong Kong, I received letters from various church members detailing the problems they were facing. This led me to judge those who had decided to move to the new church. However, one rainy day, I felt God correct me and reveal that these events were part of His greater purpose. When I returned to New Zealand for a furlough, I spoke to both congregations about this being God's plan. Many at one church disagreed, but in hindsight, we now have two thriving churches ministering to different groups of people.

The original church had supported me during my ten years of overseas mission work, so I felt a sense of loyalty and thought I should spend at least a year there out of respect. When I first started attending again, I missed the encouragement and continuous teaching I had received as an active missionary. The larger church felt dry, and I felt unfulfilled.

Initially, I felt the pastor was not spirit-filled, but that changed after he and his wife visited a church in the USA. He came back a transformed man. Gradually, I realised it was up to me to encourage and minister to others. Towards the end of that first year, I felt God was asking me to attend the larger church regularly. Occasionally, I would also visit the small church in Hūnua that had supported me overseas.

Although I had no desire for a leadership role, I soon realised that my true calling was to quietly refresh and encourage others on their spiritual journeys. God was asking me to identify the gifts others had, and to help release and encourage them to use their gifts.

I felt that God was calling me to sit in a position where I could see most of the congregation. Obeying this, I did so, and God began to reveal to me who was hurting and sometimes why. I quickly learned not to take immediate action, but instead to offer this information back to God, asking, "You have shown me this, so what do You want me to do?" Often, He would then direct me to have that person pray with the one He had pointed out. If God revealed an issue, I was not to mention it unless the person brought it up themselves, which many did. In other cases, the issue surfaced on its own later on.

Reflecting back, I'm amazed by the number of different tasks and roles I've taken on over the years. Pondering over how this was possible, my *Word for Today* showed exactly how:

Saturday, 14 December 2013

"...Stir up the gift of God... in you..." (2 Timothy 1:6 NKJV)

God gave you your talent, but it's your job to develop it. And it's not that complicated, because your gift usually relates to something that excites you. Think about it: God made you; He hardwired the desires of your heart. Knowing that helps you to understand why the things you find rewarding involve your innate talents and abilities.

One author says: "It's natural for a hunting dog to hunt. Coop him up and he'll lie around with no enthusiasm. But when he realises he's going hunting, he comes alive. That's because God designed hunting dogs that way. They have that passion inside them... They don't have to get themselves worked up... or say, 'Let me go listen to a sermon or motivational message so I can work up some zest and zeal.' No, when those dogs know they're going hunting they're naturally excited... And when we're doing what we know we're called to do, enthusiasm and excitement exude from us naturally. We may not jump up and down... but deep within, we know, 'This is what I was called to do. This is why I was born.' On the other hand, if you're doing something that's not natural, it's a struggle. If you try, train, practice and push and you still can't master a skill; recognise that it may not be in your nature. Of course we must persevere... push through and learn hard things... but in general, life shouldn't be a constant struggle."

> When you're fulfilling your purpose, one of the most noticeable results is how rewarding it feels to "stir up the gift of God... in you" by utilising your natural abilities.[9]

I was asked to assist at several Alpha courses, which proved to be a very rewarding experience as I witnessed others grow in their faith. My brother Ron had attended one. Alpha courses are designed for non-Christians, with the aim of encouraging participants to deepen their spiritual understanding. Many of the attendees subsequently became involved in church leadership in various capacities.

After attending an Alpha course, I felt compelled to lead the group that had participated. However, I believed my leadership should be limited to no more than a year. I asked the minister for permission, and he approved. Later, I learned there was a formal process that required coordinating with other home group leaders, and they were upset that I had established a group without their awareness or approval. Despite this, the group thrived.

At one time I was feeling very spiritually drained. A friend then recommended I attend a "Walk to Emmaus" retreat, a 72-hour Christian spiritual renewal experience. The retreat focused on prayer, meditation, and worship. I found the principles, based on Luke 24:13-45, to be deeply refreshing, helping me refocus on God. It was inspiring to witness God working through the other attendees as well.

Prior to my missionary work, the church I attended held four Sunday services. An 8 am communion service was followed by a traditional 9.15 am service and a more contemporary 10.45 am service. Sunday concluded with an evening worship service. These spirit-filled gatherings often featured prophecies, tongues, and interpretations, which were generally quite fulfilling for the congregation.

I have always said my house belongs to God, and I have a good friend, Claire Simpson, who used to bring students from YWAM to visit and stay on the farm. Duncan Whitty, the engineer from *Africa Mercy*, knew Claire from Scotland and had sent her to see me in New Zealand. I really enjoyed this, and she knew I loved to tell stories as a way of teaching God's word. I love to be able to encourage others, and the more visitors I can entertain, the happier I am.

Yea, though I walk through the valley of the shadow of death,
I will fear no evil;
For You are with me;
Your rod and Your staff, they comfort me.
(Psalm 23:4)

In 2014 I had a heart attack and was whisked off to hospital with the ambulance travelling along the winding road from the farm at Hūnua almost as fast as "Jim-Speed." Whilst this was an extremely worrying time for my family, once in hospital, I was unconcerned. When my middle daughter called shortly before my quadruple bypass surgery, she asked if I was ok, and I replied, "I have made my peace with God." If He were to take me then, I was ready to go.

Clearly I hadn't finished my chores, as I am still here writing this!

TEN
FINAL THOUGHTS

Now also when I am old and grayheaded,
O God, do not forsake me,
Until I declare Your strength to this generation,
Your power to everyone who is to come.
(Psalm 71:18)

Growing up I considered my childhood was fairly normal, but I realise now that the wide range of experiences I had meant that I was willing to try out all sorts of different experiences later in life, particularly in the service of God. New Zealanders (Kiwis) are well known for their innovative and "fix anything" attitudes and these are qualities I carried through to all my different mission experiences.

My own father humbled and taught me about daily prayer, that led me to have a greater understanding of how you can quietly go about God's business without anyone even knowing. And it was only much later in life that I realised the impact of the Billy Graham crusade on me, and I have learned that sometimes the biggest changes in someone may not be revealed on the outside until many years later.

My time in the Young Farmers, Rifle and Lions Clubs were instrumental in helping with building confidence and self-belief, learning leadership qualities, public speaking in front of large groups and serving the public. Later this meant I was able to comfortably address large congregations and before serving God in mission work, I had already learnt to serve whatever community I was in.

Downsizing from a large farm to a much smaller one resulted in me gaining experiences in many other occupations like Real Estate, Auctions, and Wool Buying which all added to my pool of skills, which were useful when I moved into mission work.

The change in my personal circumstances in my fifties was God's way of drawing me closer to himself, and it was only through experiencing loss that I was able to learn about compassion and accepting help, the grace of God, and being able to freely move forward in whatever service He called me to.

Working with Mercy Missions locally in South Auckland distributing food really helped me to pray and trust in God that what we felt was truly direction from Him, and I learned what happened if we doubted his word. My early experience with "Mac" was a precursor to working with addicts in Hong Kong.

St Stephen's Society led me to Hong Kong, working in two different areas – Hang Fook Camp and Pillar Point – and gave me compassion and an understanding of what it truly means to be poor, and how challenging it can be to recover from difficult circumstances. I also saw powerful evidence of how God's grace can even make withdrawal from drug addiction a much easier process for the person involved.

My time in England gave me even more belief in how Gods provision comes about – the final cost of the *Africa Mercy* refit was over US$62 million, and like my vision, much of it came about through small donations. If you look at their web page today, you can see people around the world making small and large donations continuously.

Since my return home I have focused on being the Encourager. I want to inspire people to have a go at mission work or encourage them in their Christian faith. I continue to wear my Mercy Ships jersey so people can ask me questions about it. I proudly wear it as a reminder of my time on the ship. In the same way that my Recycled Teen T-shirt gave others a smile, my blue jersey is symbolic of what has given me the most joy in the service of God.

ACKNOWLEDGEMENTS

I started writing this book almost thirty years ago after I returned from mission work in Hong Kong. Many people have been involved along my journey, and I cannot possibly acknowledge every one of them, but I thank you all.

I first must acknowledge God for his hand in my life. Without whom none of this would have happened. To Carol, my daughters, and my parents who gave me life experiences that have shaped this journey and I will forever be grateful for.

I would like to acknowledge the input from my wider family, many of whom have passed on. In my early years, our neighbours, friends, and teachers. My time at Kings College in Ōtāhuhu, while it was initially difficult, taught me how to get on with people. My headmaster, Mr Greenbank, who had more faith in me than I had in myself. His college staff all had an input into my life. Also, I would like to especially mention Mark Hanna, who was memorable and helpful tutor at Selwyn House at Kings College.

I would also like to thank the Young Farmers Club for the training and leadership they instilled in me. I would like to acknowledge the late John Garret who taught me to weld, and how to relate to electricity without killing myself. His teaching has stood me in good stead all my life, and gave me skills to use while in active missionary service.

I would like to thank the people of Kopaki and Te Kūiti for all their encouragement, with special mention of Ray Derby and Dawn Grainger. Also to Neil Burndred, who at the time worked for Marine Helicopters, and much later became my very good neighbour at Hūnua. Then to Rik van Miltenburg, Graeme Kelly, Graeme Chitty, Mary and Derek Graham, John Balchin, Bruce Benge, Rex and Barbara Stone, George and Hazel Allen.

While I was in Hong Kong, Jackie Pullinger and her staff who made me feel welcome, Weymond Fong, Hayley Graham, who led the New Boy House. James and Belinder Ginns, Martin Sperring, Dermot Stack, Peter Emmet and others who worked in the Vietnamese Refugee camp.

In England, at Youth With A Mission in Harpenden. Lynn Green, Ken Hudson and his wife Mary, John Clark and his wife Val all provided valuable friendship and support.

At Mercy Ships, Donovan and Mae Palmer, Geoff Morgan, Captain Ben Wooley, Jim Paterson, Lubbert Veenstra, Tamara Goodwin, David Millar, Frank van Eck and Dave Roderick. They all supported me and taught me many new things.

And finally, special thanks to the team in the Mercy Ships office in Auckland for providing photos we could use for the cover of this book.

Knowing myself I have probably missed so many more, and I ask your forgiveness for that, but know that you all hold a special place in my heart.

NOTES

1. Jackie Pullinger, www.ststephenssociety.com/about-us
2. Ibid.
3. Ibid.
4. Hong Kong Tourism Board, www.discoverhongkong.com
5. www.ywam.org/about-us/history
6. www.mercyships.org.au/wp-content/uploads/2021/10/Mercy-Ships-Our-Ships-History.pdf
7. www.mercyships.dk/wp-content/uploads/2024/07/SOM.pdf)
8. Ibid.
9. Bob and Debby Gass, *Word for Today*

Additional Bible versions quoted:

Scripture quotations marked AMP are taken from the Amplified Bible, Copyright © 1954, 1958, 1962, 1964, 1965, 1987 by The Lockman Foundation. Used by permission.

Scripture quotations marked KJV are taken from The Authorized (King James) Version. Rights in the Authorized Version in the United Kingdom are vested in the Crown. Public domain in New Zealand.

Scripture quotations marked NIV are taken from the Holy Bible, New International Version®, NIV®. Copyright © 1973, 1978, 1984, 2011 by Biblica, Inc.™ Used by permission of Zondervan. All rights reserved worldwide.

www.ingramcontent.com/pod-product-compliance
Lightning Source LLC
Chambersburg PA
CBHW051438290426
44109CB00016B/1609